WRITING TO LEARN:
FROM PARAGRAPH TO ESSAY

An Intermediate Writing Textbook

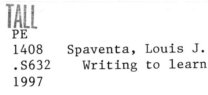

WRITING TO LEARN:

FROM PARAGRAPH TO ESSAY

An Intermediate Writing Textbook

LOUIS J. SPAVENTA

MARILYNN L. SPAVENTA
Santa Barbara City College

St. Martin's Press
New York

Sponsoring Editor: *Tina B. Carver*
Editorial Assistant: *Karen George*
Manager, Publishing Services: *Emily Berleth*
Publishing Services Associate: *Meryl Perrin*
Project Management: *Tünde A. Dewey/Dewey Publishing Services*
Production Supervisor: *Scott Lavelle*
Text Design: *Dewey Publishing Services*
Illustrations: *Peter Bono*
Photos: *Bill Morrison*
Cover Design: *Evelyn Horovicz*
Cover Art: *Peter Bono*

Library of Congress Catalog Card Number: 95-73194

Manufactured in the United States of America.

1 0 9 8 7
f e d c b

For information, write:
St. Martin's Press
175 Fifth Avenue
New York, NY 10010

ISBN: 0-312-13729-X

CONTENTS

TO THE TEACHER   xi

TO THE STUDENT   xiv

UNIT ONE: MYSELF AND OTHERS   2

PART I — PREWRITING   3
Activity 1: Brainstorming   3
Activity 2: Writing Definitions   3

PART II — STRUCTURE   4
Activity 1: Present and Past Tense Review   4
Activity 2: Uniformity in Tense   6
Activity 3: Verb plus Verb   6

PART III — WRITING AND EDITING   8
Activity 1: Note Writing   8
Activity 2: Editing Titles   9
Activity 3: Writing Titles   10
Activity 4: Limiting the Topic by Editing   10
Activity 5: Limiting the Topic by Grouping   11
Activity 6: Writing a Topic Sentence   13
Activity 7: Staying with the Topic   14

PART IV — WRITING AND REVISING ASSIGNMENT   15

ADDITIONAL PRACTICE   16
  A. Note Writing (Prewriting)   16
  B. Writing More about Yourself (Structure)   17
  C. Practice with Past and Present Tenses (Structure) 18
  D. Rewriting (Structure/Writing)   18
  E. Titles (Editing)   19
  F. Titles (Editing)   20
  G. Paragraph Form (Editing)   21
  H. Topic Sentence (Editing)   21
  I. Grammar Review: Using Pronouns in a
      Paragraph (Structure)   22
      Personal Pronoun Review Chart   24
  J. Paragraph Writing (Writing)   25

UNIT ONE JOURNAL TOPIC SUGGESTIONS   26

UNIT ONE VOCABULARY LOG   27

UNIT TWO: FAMILY AND RELATIONSHIPS

28

PART I — PREWRITING 29
Activity 1: Making Connections 29
Activity 2: Freewriting 29
Activity 3: Identifying Family Members 30

PART II — STRUCTURE 31
Activity 1: Using Commas in a Series 31
Activity 2: Combining Sentences with Coordinating
Conjunctions: *and, but, so,* and *or* 32
Sentence Combining Chart: Unit 2 33

PART III — WRITING AND EDITING 35
Activity 1: Sentence Combining Editing 35
Activity 2: Editing for Punctuation 35

PART IV — WRITING AND REVISING ASSIGNMENT 36

ADDITIONAL PRACTICE 36
A. Writing a Story (Writing) 36
B. Relationship Vocabulary (Vocabulary) 37
C. Talking about Family (Prewriting) 38
D. Writing about the Future (Writing) 38
E. Identifying Subjects and Verbs (Structure) 38
F. Combining Sentences with Coordinating
Conjunctions (Editing) 39
G. Using Commas Correctly (Editing) 40
H. Editing a Story with Coordinating Conjunctions (Editing) 40
I. Writing Titles and Topic Sentences (Writing) 41

UNIT TWO JOURNAL TOPIC SUGGESTIONS 42

UNIT TWO VOCABULARY LOG 43

UNIT THREE: EDUCATION

44

PART I — PREWRITING 45
Activity 1: Building an Argument 45
Activity 2: Group Writing Using Transitions 45
Activity 3: Peer Editing 46

PART II — STRUCTURE 47
Activity 1: Organizing by Location Using Prepositional Phrases 47
Activity 2: Remembering Your Classroom 48

Activity 3: Joining Sentences with Subordinating
                Conjunctions of Time   50

Activity 4: Using Subordinating Conjunctions of Time   53

Activity 5: More Subordinating Conjunctions   54

               Sentence Combining Chart: Unit 3   54

               Sentence Combining Chart: Example Sentences   55

PART III — WRITING AND EDITING   57

Activity 1: Recognizing and Changing Sentence Fragments
               into Sentences   57

Activity 2: Recognizing Fragments   57

Activity 3: Editing for Sentence Fragments   59

PART IV — WRITING AND REVISING ASSIGNMENTS   60

ADDITIONAL PRACTICE   63

A. Prepositions of Location (Structure)   63

B. Prepositions of Location (Structure/Vocabulary)   64

C. Freewriting (Prewriting)   66

D. Identifying Dependent and Independent Clauses (Structure)   67

E. Editing Sentence Fragments (Structure/Editing)   67

F. Academic Vocabulary (Vocabulary)   69

G. Writing a Paragraph of Description (Writing)   70

H. Writing Descriptive Sentences (Prewriting/Writing)   71

I. Informal Letter Writing/Giving Advice (Writing)   72

UNIT THREE JOURNAL TOPIC SUGGESTIONS   74

UNIT THREE VOCABULARY LOG   75

UNIT FOUR: WORK   76

PART I — PREWRITING   77

Activity 1: Discussing the Picture   77

Activity 2: Discussing Your Job   77

Activity 3: Brainstorming/Vocabulary   78

Activity 4: Expressing Relationships   78

Activity 5: Vocabulary   79

Activity 6: Freewriting   80

PART II — STRUCTURE   81

Activity 1: Connecting Sentences with Transitions: *therefore*
               and *however*   81

               Sentence Combining Chart: Unit 4   82

               Sentence Combining Chart: Example Sentences   82

Activity 2: Practice with *so* and *but*   84

Activity 3: From Spoken to Written English   84
Activity 4: Recognizing Run-on Sentences   84

PART III — WRITING AND EDITING   86
Activity 1: Interview Research   86
Activity 2: Editing Questions and Answers   87

PART IV — WRITING AND REVISING ASSIGNMENT   88

ADDITIONAL PRACTICE   92
A. Sample Advertisement and Job Application Letter (Prewriting)   92
B. Identifying Sentences (Structure)   95
C. Application Vocabulary (Vocabulary)   96
D. Preparing for an Interview (Writing/Vocabulary)   97
E. Story (Structure)   98
F. Informal Letter Writing (Writing)   99

UNIT FOUR JOURNAL TOPIC SUGGESTIONS   100

UNIT FOUR VOCABULARY LOG   101

UNIT FIVE: LEISURE AND RECREATION   102

PART I — PREWRITING   103
Activity 1: Vocabulary Warm-Up   103
Activity 2: Talking about Leisure Activities   104
Activity 3: Freewriting   104
Activity 4: Sorting or Categorizing   105
Activity 5: Writing a First Draft   108

PART II — STRUCTURE   109
Activity 1: Writing Transition Sentences   109
Activity 2: Using *such as, for example,* and *for instance*   109

PART III — WRITING AND EDITING   111
Activity 1: Writing with *such as, for example,* and *for instance*   111
Activity 2: Editing Sentence Fragments with *such as, for example,* and *for instance*   112
Activity 3: Writing Sentences with *such as, for example,* and *for instance*   113
Activity 4: Form of an Essay   114
Activity 5: Writing the Introduction and Conclusion   116

PART IV — WRITING AND REVISING ASSIGNMENT   119

ADDITIONAL PRACTICE   120
     A. Vocabulary Expansion (Vocabulary)   120
     B. Giving Examples (Structure)   120
     C. Editing for Fragments and Run-ons: Review (Structure)   121
     D. Reading Reviews (Vocabulary)   122
     E. Writing Reviews (Writing/Vocabulary)   123

UNIT FIVE JOURNAL TOPIC SUGGESTIONS   124

UNIT FIVE VOCABULARY LOG   125

UNIT SIX: THE NATURAL WORLD   126

PART I — PREWRITING   127
Activity 1: Painting a Picture in Words   127
Activity 2: Comparing Experience   127
Activity 3: Scientific Language   127

PART II — STRUCTURE   129
Activity 1: Using *also, then,* and *on the other hand*   129
     Sentence Combining Chart: Unit 6   129
     Sentence Combining Chart: Example Sentences   130
Activity 2: Describing the Geography of Your Country   132
Activity 3: Comparing Natural Scenes   133

PART III — WRITING AND EDITING   134
Activity 1: Reading and Analyzing an Essay   134
Activity 2: Topic vs. Thesis   137
Activity 3: The Thesis   137
Activity 4: Editing an Essay   139

PART IV — WRITING AND REVISING ASSIGNMENT   142

ADDITIONAL PRACTICE   143
A. Describing (Prewriting)   143
B. Writing Descriptive Sentences (Writing)   143
C. Freewriting (Prewriting)   144
D. Using *on the other hand* (Structure)   145
E. Run-ons and Fragments (Structure and Editing)   146

UNIT SIX JOURNAL TOPIC SUGGESTIONS   147

UNIT SIX VOCABULARY LOG   148

APPENDIX ONE: SAMPLE PAPER   149

APPENDIX TWO: JOURNAL WRITING   151

APPENDIX THREE: CAPITALIZATION   152

APPENDIX FOUR: PUNCTUATION   153

APPENDIX FIVE: WRITER FEEDBACK SHEET   155

APPENDIX SIX: GLOSSARY   156

TO THE TEACHER

Writing to Learn is a three-part process and product writing series for ESL students from diverse educational backgrounds. The progression takes the student from writing good paragraphs—*Writing Paragraphs*—to a transition from paragraph to essay writing—*From Paragraph to Essay*—and finally to writing strong essays—*Writing Essays*. *Writing to Learn* makes use of student skills and experience to generate writing topics while it provides guided practice in appropriate grammar and vocabulary, English writing conventions, and writing, editing, rewriting.

Our goal in writing this series is to help our students learn how to write for academic and vocational success by using the intelligence and creativity that they bring to the classroom. We wrote the text primarily for community college ESL students, a varied group. In spite of the variety of students and their goals, there is commonality. That commonality lies in their desire to improve their writing so that they succeed at the college level.

Writing to Learn: From Paragraph to Essay leads students through the process of writing while also recognizing the importance of the product. The workbook format provides plenty of space for a great deal of practice in addition to a formal writing assignment for each unit.

Each unit in the book is divided into the following five sections:

1. Prewriting   Each unit begins with prewriting exercises that involve group and pair work, discussion, and a variety of prewriting activities including freewriting or quickwriting. We feel that it is important for students to understand writing as a process that begins with creative reflection and communication.

We also hope that students will enjoy their interaction with one another in the process of preparing to write.

2. Structure   This section focuses on grammar that students may not have yet mastered. This text is not intended to be a grammar text. The purpose of including a structure section is to reinforce the grammar that students learn at this level and to concentrate on sentence combining.

3. Writing and Editing   These exercises are meant to provide additional writing and editing practice on the topic of the unit. Each unit reviews or introduces an aspect of writing such as titles, topic sentences, and thesis.

4. Writing and Revising Assignment   Each unit presents an extensive writing assignment. The first three units require a coherent, well-organized paragraph. The third unit assigns a three-paragraph letter, and the last two units require five-paragraph essays. All these assignments should involve at least two drafts and a peer editing phase.

5. Additional Practice   These exercises offer additional practice for the prewriting, structure, and writing and editing sections in each unit. They can be assigned for homework or additional class practice at any time. Be sure to preview them before beginning each unit.

In addition to these five sections, there are also a list of journal topics and a page for entering vocabulary at the end of each unit.

Journal Topics   Students benefit from journal writing because so many of them are simply not used to writing and are not comfortable with the idea of writing. Teachers can also enjoy the opportunity to dialog with their students through their journals. If you choose to have your students keep journals, refer to the appendix on journal writing and the topic suggestions included at the end of each unit.

Vocabulary   Each unit introduces vocabulary that will help students write about the topic of the unit, thus helping them to learn new vocabulary in context. In addition, students will require other vocabulary unique to their papers. The vocabulary log at the end of each unit is the place for students to write down new words, definitions, and sample sentences for each unit, thus creating their own dictionaries.

Other Skills   All teachers like to supplement their class texts with their own favorite texts and exercises. Reading, writing, listening, and speaking should be integrated into the writing classroom ESL lesson. You, the instructor, should look through the units in the book and decide for yourself which favorite poetry, literature, music, and nonfiction pieces fit most well with the units and hold interest for your students.

Appendices   The appendices at the end of the book are a resource for both you and your students. They offer guidelines for success in college writing, a discussion of journal writing, some basic rules for capitalization and punctuation in written English, a sample writer feedback sheet, and a glossary.

Begin your classroom use of the book with an exercise that helps your students become familiar with the text. You can do this exercise orally or in writing. Students can work in pairs or in small groups.

Question your students about the names of the units, the number of sections in a unit, the location of a topic or section in a unit, the number of units and appendices, and the purpose of each unit section and appendix. Distribute a follow-up handout that describes the purpose and layout of the units, sections, and appendices.

If you do the exercise orally, use the cooperative question-and-answer technique called "numbered heads together." Have each student in a pair or group count off—1, 2, or 1, 2, 3, 4. Tell the class that before you call on anyone, a student that knows the answer should tell it to his or her partner or group. When you call "number 1," the number 1 students raise their hands. Call on a student. If a student's answer is correct, go on to the next question. If the answer is not correct, ask another number 1 student. In this way, you can begin teaching pair or group work, an essential element of the writing process in *Writing to Learn: From Paragraph to Essay,* and you can help students familiarize themselves with the text.

TEACHERS' MANUAL

The teachers' manual for *Writing to Learn: From Paragraph to Essay* includes supporting materials for the text. These should be especially useful for part-time instructors. The manual includes:

- reproducible pages of editing exercises and examples of student-generated work
- suggestions for working with each unit
- reproducible quizzes for each unit
- reproducible final structure test

We enjoy teaching with this book, and we have seen that our students enjoy learning with it. We hope you and your students will have similar positive experiences.

Acknowledgments

First and most of all, we wish to thank our students at Santa Barbara City College and Allan Hancock College; this book came from them and is written for them. The comments and suggestions from our colleagues have been very helpful in revising the text. We give special thanks to Frank Lazorchik, who has a keen eye for details, and to Teresa Jamison and Tara Cloud, who have been very supportive. Julie Alpert added her drawings to our initial manuscript for the book. Peter Bono contributed his drawings, and Bill Morrison did an excellent job of producing photos.

We would also like to thank the following St. Martin's Press reviewers for their comments and suggestions: Leslie Barratt, Indiana State University; Karen Einstein, Santa Rosa Junior College; Veronica L. Gouvea, Roxbury Community College; Heidimarie Hayes Rambo, Kent State University; and Doug Woken, University of Illinois.

The layout of the book benefited from the professional guidance of Tünde A. Dewey. The project could not have come to a successful conclusion without the enthusiasm of Ed Stanford, Tina Carver, and Emily Berleth of St. Martin's Press. We thank everyone for their help.

Should you have any suggestions or comments, we would be happy to receive them from you. You can write to us care of the ESL Department, Santa Barbara City College, 721 Cliff Drive, Santa Barbara, CA, 93109.

Lou and Marilynn Spaventa
Santa Barbara, CA

TO THE STUDENT

Welcome to ***Writing to Learn: From Paragraph to Essay!***
The goal of this book is to help you write good paragraphs and good essays. The first part of the book concentrates on paragraph writing and the second part, on essay writing. The book is divided into six units. Each unit has a topic for discussion and writing. The topic of Unit One is: Myself and Others. Look for the topics of the other units in the Table of Contents and write them below.

Unit One: Myself and Others _____

Unit Two: _____

Unit Three: _____

Unit Four: _____

Unit Five: _____

Unit Six: _____

If you think a little about these topics, you will find that they progress from things that you know well and that are somewhat private—yourself and your family—to things that you often share publicly with others—education, jobs, how you spend your free time, and the world around you. While we feel that writing about what you know is a good way to become a proficient writer, we also feel that it is necessary to keep learning more in order to write better. Therefore, as you work with this book, you will be asked to use ideas and information that may be new to you. Using new ideas and information is part of what you must learn to do in order to succeed in other courses that do not focus on learning to write in English.

Each unit in the book is divided into the following sections:

- *Prewriting*—These activities are designed to help you think about, discuss, and write down ideas about the unit topic.

- *Structure*—These exercises are designed to help you review and practice grammar that you can use in your writing.

- *Writing and Editing*—These practices focus on language to help you improve your writing.

- *Writing and Revising*—This assignment is the principal writing task that you will work on when you study the unit.

- *Additional Practice*—This section offers more activities and ideas for writing.

Your instructor will decide what order and which activities are best for you and your classmates. You may do all the activities in a unit, or you may do only some of them. This is particularly true for the *Additional Practice* section.

This book will help you move from writing good paragraphs to writing good essays. What is a good paragraph and what is a good essay? Most students would say that the teacher is the best judge of what is good. However, we believe that you also know what is good writing and what is writing that needs more work. One other goal of this book is to help you see that writing is both a process and a product. While just about anything that is written can be improved—yes, even your instructor's writing—at some point the writer must say, "For now this is the best I can make this piece of writing." But to say this, you first need to work hard at making your writing better. It takes time and practice, just like developing any other skill, whether it is learning to cook or learning to play the piano.

WRITING TO LEARN:

FROM PARAGRAPH TO ESSAY

An Intermediate Writing Textbook

UNIT ONE

MYSELF AND OTHERS

PART I — PREWRITING

Activity 1: Brainstorming

Think about how many times you pick up a pencil or pen every day to write in your first language. How many different kinds of writing are there?

Work in groups of three. Only one student needs to write, but *everyone* should give ideas. Don't worry about spelling. Don't write in complete sentences. Write as many ideas as your group can think of in four minutes.

EXAMPLE:

1. letters to friends
2. pay bills
3. shopping list
4.
5.
6.

When you finish, exchange your information with other groups by reading aloud your list, or by writing it on the board.

Did you get new ideas from your groups?
Did you get even more ideas from the class?

Activity 2: Writing Definitions

What you just did in *Activity 1* is called **brainstorming**. Can you write a short definition of *brainstorming*?

Hint: One way to write a definition is by using the **-ING** form of the verb.

Brainstorming is

_____ -ing _____ .

(my definition)

Compare your definition with the definitions of other class members.

Brainstorming is _____ .

(class definition)

Now, write your definition on page 27, in your Vocabulary log.

Did you write a better definition after hearing other students' ideas?

PART II — STRUCTURE

Activity 1: Present and Past Tense Review

Grammar Review: It is important to use verb tenses correctly.

> ### USES OF THE SIMPLE PRESENT TENSE
>
> 1. The present tense is used to express habits:
>   *Lou practices guitar every day.*
>
> 2. It is used to talk about things that do not change:
>   *The sun rises in the east.*
>
> 3. It is used to describe people and things with the verb **be**:
>   *Marilynn is the mother of three children.*
>
> 4. It is used with words that express future time when we talk about
>   a plan or a list of activities that we will do in the future.
>   *Thursday we fly to Las Vegas and we return on Sunday.*

There are other uses of the present tense, but we will not review them here.

A. Use the words to make a sentence with the simple present tense of the verb. Remember that there are many irregular verbs.

EXAMPLE: deliver, newspapers, every morning

My brother delivers newspapers every morning.

1. (I), jog, three miles, every afternoon

   _____

2. sun, set, in the west

   _____

3. Pablo, be, a professor

   _____

4. John, love, tennis

   _____

5. hot air, rise

   _____

6. Professor Ross, teach, physics

   _____

7. the earth, be, round

_____

8. Tomorrow, we, finish, the first chapter

_____

USES OF THE SIMPLE PAST TENSE

1. The simple past tense is used for an event or action that has finished at a definite time in the past:
   a. *Kate returned from her trip yesterday.*
   b. *Lou worked for the federal government.*

2. In a sentence like 1b, the meaning usually is that the fact or event is no longer true. In this case, Lou probably *does not work* for the federal government now. Therefore, this sentence is similar to one using *used to*.
   Lou used to work for the federal government.

There are other uses of the simple past tense, but we will not review them here.

B. Use the words to make a sentence. Use the simple past tense of the verb. Remember that there are many irregular verbs.

EXAMPLE: Pat, prepare, a dish, for the party

    Pat prepared a dish for the party.

1. Roberto, hand out, the homework

_____

2. Gail, run, in a marathon race

_____

3. Maria, teach, kindergarten

_____

4. Julie, work, in Spain

_____

5. Keiko, be, a waitress

_____

6. Kim and Truong, be, refugees

_____

7. Men, land, on the moon, in 1969

_____

8. The Rangers, win, the Stanley Cup, in 1994

_____

9. Women in the United States, vote, for the first time, in 1920

_____

_____

10. Peter, graduate, from Harvard University, 25 years ago

_____

_____

Activity 2: Uniformity in Tense

Read this paragraph. Notice that there are sentences using both the past and the present tenses. Try to change as many as possible to present tense. There may be some that cannot be changed.

An Outdoor Person

Gail is a person who loves to be outdoors. She is very athletic and she skied a lot. She often went to her uncle's to ski in the mountains. Skiing was not her only outdoor interest. Gail also loved to run and play tennis. However, a couple of years ago, she had a knee operation. Because of this, she had to stop running marathons. These days Gail's knee is much better and she could play tennis as much as she wants to. She also could run, but not in marathon races. Gail loves to be active outdoors. California is the perfect place for her because the sun always shined here.

Activity 3: Verb plus Verb

Many students have problems writing sentences when there is a verb after a verb. The first verb can be in any tense. The second verb is either the **TO** form (**infinitive**) or the **-ING** form (**gerund**). There is no rule; the second verb is determined by the first verb. You have to learn these combinations by practice or memorization.

EXAMPLE: **want**   *I want to learn more English this year.*
enjoy   *I enjoy learning languages.*
like   *I like to learn new things.*   OR
I like learning new things.

Here are some common verbs you may need for your writing assignments. There are many more. Most intermediate to advanced level grammar books contain complete lists.

Verbs that take -**ING** (gerund)	Verbs that take **TO** (infinitive)	Verbs that take -**ING** or **TO** (gerund or infinitive)
admit	agree	begin
appreciate	ask	continue
discuss	come	forget*
dislike	decide	hate
enjoy	hope	like
finish	learn	love
don't mind	need	plan
miss	offer	prefer
suggest	promise	remember*
understand	want	start
		stop*
		try*

* There is a meaning difference between *verb* + **to** and *verb* + -**ing.**

Use the verbs to write sentences about yourself. The first verb can be in any tense. The second verb must be an infinitive or gerund form.

EXAMPLE: enjoy, attend
    I enjoy attending classes because I meet new people.

1. finish, do

_____

2. suggest, go

_____

3. hope, learn

_____

4. want, visit

_____

5. hate, see

_____

6. love, eat

_____

7. don't mind, work

_____

8. continue, study

_____

9. started, walk

_____

10. decide, buy

_____

PART III — WRITING AND EDITING

Activity 1: Note Writing

Writing is an important way of communicating. Would you like to try to communicate in writing with your new classmates? Let's try it.

For the next 20 minutes, write to as many classmates as possible. Don't forget your teacher!

- write *short* messages
- introduce yourself *or* ask questions *or* give information
- sign your notes
- fold each note, then get up and deliver it
- answer the notes you receive
- don't worry about mistakes

There's only one important rule: **Don't talk at all!** Work fast. This should be fun! You'll get practice writing and get to know your classmates at the same time.

EXAMPLES:

Hi! What's your name? What country do you come from? You are so quiet. Are you shy?

Mario

I like the shirt you're wearing today.

Svetlana

Activity 2: Editing Titles

Titles *are not* complete sentences in English. When you write titles in English, follow these rules:

- Capitalize the first word.
- Capitalize all words except articles (*a, an, the,* etc.) and prepositions (*to, from, at,* etc.). Pronouns are usually capitalized.
- Remember that countries, languages, and people from countries are always capitalized (American, French, Korean, etc.).
- Titles are short, and some words are missing.
- Don't use a period (.) at the end, but you may need a question mark (?) or an exclamation mark (!).
- Don't use quotation marks ("…").
- Center a title.

EXAMPLES: Meet Takahiro
Amazing Alfredo
A Student with a Dream

Write the following titles with correct capitalization and punctuation.

EXAMPLE: welcome to this class
Welcome to This Class

1. the girl from costa rica

   _____

2. gloria's goal

   _____

3. a hardworking young man from guatemala

   _____

4. a man with big plans

   _____

5. alone but not lonely

   _____

6. susie's surprise

   _____

7. shy or respectful

   _____

8. from mexico city to chicago

   _____

Activity 3: Writing Titles

When you write a paragraph or an essay, you need to have a **main idea** or **point of view**. That is the **focus**. Writing a title can help you **focus**. Don't forget that a title should be interesting, too. You want to get your reader's attention even before he or she begins to read your paragraph or essay.

Read this paragraph, and then choose the best title from below.

> Luis likes to study, but he loves to play soccer. When he was a boy, his father always told him, "Study hard and get a good education." Luis listened to his father. He always studied hard and got good grades, but he was happier when he was kicking a soccer ball around the field. Now his father is very proud of him because he is a student at City College. Luis plays on the college soccer team, too. He is happy because he can do both of the things he loves.

Which is the best title? (Which title shows the **focus**?) Why?

1. Luis Comes from Argentina
2. Luis
3. A Student and a Soccer Player

Now read this paragraph. After you have read it, write a title for it. Then compare your title with your classmates' titles.

> When you first see Takahiro, you think he is a typical student. This is only half true. Takahiro is a student, but he is not typical. In fact, I was very surprised when I talked to him. Takahiro was in the army in his country. He was a special forces soldier and a judo expert. He liked his life in the army, but he wanted a change. Now he is a student at City College. When you see Takahiro, talk to him. Everyone will want to be his friend. Maybe everybody will be a little afraid of him, too!

Activity 4: Limiting the Topic by Editing

After you brainstorm or make notes for a paragraph, you have to decide on your **focus**, or main idea. When you do that, you have to cut out or delete some information. For example, if you are writing only one paragraph about someone, you can't write that person's whole life story.

Look at these notes for a paragraph about a student named Daniel. Make groups of the related information. You can do this in several ways. Some people like to **circle similar ideas**, while others **rewrite them in columns**. Still other people **use numbers** to code categories or **make a map** to show the relationships.

Choose one of these methods, and group the information in a more focused way.

Daniel

born in 1973   hardworking   goal = accountant   likes basketball
enjoys writing letters to his family
mother died in 1980   5 siblings live in Mexico   serious
attended 1 year at university in Mexico City   8 brothers and sisters   athletic
likes dancing   studied French for 1 year   3 brothers live in the U.S.
wants to marry his girlfriend soon   brother helping him with money now
family gets together every Christmas

How many possible paragraphs could you write about Daniel? How did you **limit the topic** "Daniel"? Are there more questions you would ask Daniel before writing a paragraph about him?

Activity 5: Limiting the Topic by Grouping

Look at these notes about an ESL teacher. Group the related ideas. Cross out any notes that are not related. Practice two methods of organizing. First, group by writing categories in the chart that follows. Because there are different ways of thinking, it is possible for you to put an idea in a different category than your classmate does. Both ways can be right.

Then practice filling in the map that follows the chart.

Gail

loves teaching people from other countries... loyalty to friends and family is very important for her... loves to ski, play tennis... has visited 4 continents and 20 countries... went to high school in Pasadena, California... likes to spend vacation traveling to far off places... had a happy and active childhood with 2 older brothers... went to a very small college in New York/liked it, but too cold... doesn't attend a traditional church... loved art and theater in college... didn't like to study in college... values family and friends... has run in several marathons... transferred from New York college to UCLA... one time in college she got a "D" in a course because she went to a political protest instead of class... went to France for 1 semester in college... swam in college but didn't do any sports... was interested in politics in college... attended graduate school in Vermont with students from all over the world... loves challenge and adventure... loves her family... likes to spend holidays with family... wants to travel in the future... especially wants to visit all the countries in Africa... loves cats

A. Chart

Gail's Pastimes and Interests	Gail's Education	Gail's International Interests

B. Map

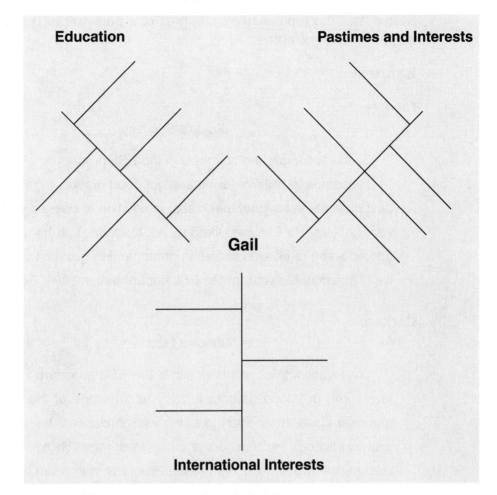

Education

Pastimes and Interests

Gail

International Interests

Activity 6: Writing a Topic Sentence

A **topic sentence** is the sentence in the paragraph that gives the main idea or the writer's opinion. Like the title, it often shows the **focus** of the paragraph. It often comes at the beginning of the paragraph. Like the title, a topic sentence should be interesting.

Read the following paragraph about an ESL teacher. Write a title and a topic sentence for it.

_____

_____ . His first experience in another country was on a beautiful island south of Korea. It was such a wonderful experience that he decided to live and work in other parts of the world, too. As a graduate student, he lived and worked in Mexico. He taught in Saudi Arabia next. Everything about his life was different there. Then he went back to Korea, but this time to the capital city, Seoul. After that, he lived in Hawaii. Although Hawaii is part of the United States, it is very different from New York, where he grew up. His travels continued to Yugoslavia, England, and Barbados. Now he's teaching me here. I wonder if he feels at home.

Notice that the topic sentence is part of a paragraph. It is usually *not* a separate paragraph.

EXAMPLE:

Incorrect

Josue's Success

Josue accomplished his goals in the ESL program.

He completed all five levels and got good grades. In fact, he was one of the best students in his grammar class. In addition to doing well in classes, he was very popular. He was well liked by his teachers and his classmates. He even tutored some of his classmates in grammar. His greatest success was when he was student of the year for the ESL department in 1994. Congratulations Josue!

Correct

Josue's Success

Josue accomplished his goals in the ESL program. He completed all five levels and got good grades. In fact, he was one of the best students in his grammar class. In addition to doing well in classes, he was very popular. He was well liked by his teachers and his classmates. He even tutored some of his classmates in grammar. His greatest success was when he was student of the year for the ESL department in 1994. Congratulations Josue!

Activity 7: Staying with the Topic

When you write a paragraph, be sure that all of the ideas and sentences are **focused** or related to the **topic sentence**.

Read this paragraph. Circle the topic sentence. Underline the sentence that does not belong in this paragraph.

Carlo and His Camera

Carlo has always wanted to be a professional photographer. He got his first camera for his seventh birthday. When he was in high school, he took photographs for the school newspaper. Although he takes pictures of everything, he especially likes to photograph people. He speaks two languages besides Italian. Carlo plans to study photography at Brooks Photography Institute after his English improves. His dream is to publish a book of photographs of famous people.

PART IV — WRITING AND REVISING ASSIGNMENT

Writing Assignment: Writing about a Classmate

Step 1: Find a partner you don't know. Write 20 *interesting* questions to ask that person. Avoid asking questions like "What is your name? How old are you? Where do you come from?"

Step 2: Spend 20 minutes together. Introduce yourself. Your partner can ask you his or her questions. Then your partner can introduce himself or herself, and you can ask your questions. When you find out something interesting, ask additional questions on that topic to find out more details. ***Don't write anything during the interview.***

Step 3: In five minutes, write down everything you can remember about your partner. Don't write in complete sentences. Don't worry about mistakes.

Step 4: Meet with your partner again. Your partner should read what you wrote and can make corrections. You can ask more questions.

Step 5: Organize your notes in a chart or map.

Step 6: Find a **focus** or main idea. You cannot write the life story of your partner in one paragraph! Write the focus in a few words. (*Example:* Takahiro is not the way he looks.)

Step 7: Write a **title** and **topic sentence**.

Step 8: Write a paragraph about your partner.

Revising Assignment

Step 1: You and your partner need to work with another pair. Exchange your paragraphs with your new partners.

Step 2: Read the paragraph from your new partner. Underline the topic sentence.

Step 3: Make sure that all the sentences are related to the topic sentence. If there is a sentence that is not related, ask your partner to explain why it is in the paragraph. Maybe she or he will want to cut it.

Step 4: If you need or want to make changes in your paragraph, rewrite it.

ADDITIONAL PRACTICE

A. Note Writing (Prewriting)

Write a note or short letter to your teacher introducing yourself. Answer **some** of these questions about yourself. Write in paragraph form.

Are you a new student or a continuing student?
How do you feel in the class? (comfortable? shy? nervous?)
What do you hope to accomplish this semester?
Do you think of yourself as a good student?
Who do you live with?
What are your special interests?
What is something about yourself that nobody else in the class knows?

B. Writing More about Yourself (Structure)

Here is a list of common activities. Write ten sentences about yourself using these words and the list of verbs that take -**ING** (page 7, verb chart, columns 1 and 3).

EXAMPLE: (column 1) I usually enjoy driving in the country.
                      (column 3) I like cooking dinner for my family.

cooking	dancing	taking a nap	driving
writing	getting married	cleaning	studying
commuting	walking	talking	reading
teaching	learning	traveling	making money

1. _____

_____

2. _____

_____

3. _____

_____

4. _____

_____

5. _____

_____

6. _____

_____

7. _____

_____

8. _____

_____

9. _____

_____

10. _____

_____

C. Practice with Past and Present Tenses (Structure)

In the story, there are several errors in tense. Some of the verbs that are in the present should be in the past tense. Some of the verbs that are in the past should be in the present tense. Some of the verbs are used correctly. Read the story and change the verbs that you need to change.

Irma and Hilario

Irma was 21 years old. She studies English every night in an adult education program. Her brother Hilario studied, too. Irma and Hilario come from Zacatecas, Mexico. Their parents still lived there, but all their brothers and sisters live in the United States. Irma likes to write in English, but Hilario didn't. He prefers just learning to speak better. Now he worked as a gardener for a big landscaping company. Hilario says that he just needs to speak and to understand English. Irma did not agree with Hilario. She thinks writing is important. She wanted to study English and to enter a university in the future. Hilario enjoys working as a gardener. He wants to own his own business one day.

D. Rewriting (Structure/Writing)

First, read the story. Then, rewrite it to make it true for you.

Things I Used to Do

When I was little, I used to walk to school. Every day my mother would make my lunch and I would carry it to school in a lunchbox. I used to meet my friends on the corner and walk with them. I liked walking with them. I wasn't used to walking by myself. When I went to junior high school, I had to get used to something new; I had to get used to taking the bus to school. It was a new experience for me, and it was hard to get used to because I had to worry about carrying the exact change for bus fare.

Now, rewrite the story. Follow the sentence patterns as they appear in the sample story, but write the story so it is true for you.

E. Titles (Editing)

These titles all have mistakes. Correct them.

1. A woman from hong kong.

2. Keiko loves america!

3. Alicias big idea

_____

4. Why Is John Happy

_____

5. "a mother and a student"

_____

6. what a great guy

_____

7. hiro the hero

_____

8. A new life in massachusetts.

_____

F. Titles (Editing)

Change these sentences into titles.

1. Jur Lie looks shy, but she is really a friendly person.

_____

2. Yukiko is a very good athlete.

_____

3. Marie plans to become a teacher.

_____

4. Kyuong-A fell in love in Chicago.

_____

5. Evaristo is a student in the daytime but a baker at night.

_____

G. Paragraph Form (Editing)

Write the following sentences in paragraph form.

Lovely Damaris Damaris is one of my nicest classmates. She always has a smile on her face and a kind word. She learns everybody's name quickly and always remembers to greet them. Damaris usually sits in front of the class so that she can concentrate. Maybe she likes to smile at the teacher, too.

_____

_____

_____

_____

_____

_____

_____

_____

H. Topic Sentence (Editing)

Read this paragraph. Rewrite it, putting the sentences in the best order. One sentence is not related to the focus. Do not include it. Underline the topic sentence.

An Actor in the Making

He studied acting for two years in France. He's a very handsome man, too, so I can imagine him starring in a romantic movie. He thinks the United States is a wonderful place for anyone to live. He knows that he must first improve his speaking and listening ability in English, so he likes to practice pronunciation and listening in the language laboratory. Now he wants to try acting in a new language. François wants to take acting classes after he finishes the ESL program. He loves when we do class activities that require conversations or acting.

I. Grammar Review: Using Pronouns in a Paragraph (Structure)

Read the story about Yuko Takai.

Someone Like Me

I left my hometown, Osaka, last year. I arrived in Los Angeles in spring. The weather was beautiful, but I felt very nervous. I was alone in a new place. I came to the United States to study English. I wanted to get away from Osaka. All my friends told me I was foolish. My friends worked in good companies. I had worked in a good company too, but I quit my job. I did not like my life because it was not interesting or exciting.

I started studying here last semester. Before studying here, I had studied in Los Angeles. In L.A., I did not speak much English, and I didn't learn much English. I hung out in Little Tokyo. I ate in Japanese restaurants. I went to a Japanese hair stylist. I bought the Japanese newspaper. I made friends, but they were all Japanese. None of them was like me. All of them wanted to get good jobs and return to Japan.

I left L.A. last summer, and now I live here. I don't have many Japanese friends, but I do speak and understand English better. I have made two friends who speak Spanish. One of them is like me. She gave up a good job to try something different. She wants to be a translator. The other friend is from Barcelona. He is an artist. I showed him some of my drawings. He thinks that I have talent. Both of my new friends want to change their lives.

In English, pronouns are used in place of nouns, especially, when the noun is repeated often in a paragraph.

EXAMPLE: *Yuko left L.A. last summer and now **she** lives here. **She** doesn't have many Japanese friends, but **she** does understand and speak English better.*

As the paragraph continues, the writer has to decide when to use pronouns and when to use the nouns that they stand for.

EXAMPLE: ***She** has made two friends who speak Spanish. One of **them** is like **her**. **Her** friend gave up a good job to try something different. **She** wants to be a translator. The other friend is from Barcelona. **He** is an artist. Yuko showed **him** some of **her** drawings. **He** thinks that **she** has talent. Both of Yuko's friends want to change **their** lives.*

Now, rewrite the first part of the story. Put in pronouns where you think they should go. Remember to use both nouns and pronouns to make your story interesting. Following the story, there is a chart of pronouns to help you.

Yuko left Yuko's hometown, Osaka, last year. Yuko arrived in Los Angeles in spring. The weather was beautiful, but Yuko felt very nervous. Yuko was alone in a new place. Yuko came to the United States to study English. Yuko wanted to get away from Osaka. All Yuko's friends told Yuko Yuko was foolish. Yuko's friends worked in good companies. Yuko had worked in a good company too, but Yuko quit Yuko's job. Yuko did not like Yuko's life because Yuko's life was not interesting or exciting.

Yuko started studying here last semester. Before studying here, Yuko had studied in Los Angeles. In L.A., Yuko did not speak much English, and Yuko didn't learn much English. Yuko hung out in Little Tokyo. Yuko ate in Japanese restaurants. Yuko went to a Japanese hair stylist. Yuko bought the Japanese newspaper. Yuko made friends, but Yuko's friends were all Japanese. None of Yuko's friends was like Yuko. All of Yuko's friends wanted to get good jobs and return to Japan.

PERSONAL PRONOUN REVIEW CHART

SUBJECT PRONOUNS		OBJECT PRONOUNS		POSSESSIVE ADJECTIVES		POSSESSIVE PRONOUNS	
I	we	me	us	my	our	mine	ours
you		you		your		yours	
he		him		his		his	
she	they	her	them	her	their	hers	theirs
it		it		its		its	

REFLEXIVE PRONOUNS	
myself	ourselves
yourself	yourselves
himself	
herself	themselves
itself	

Note: You do not need to use all of these pronouns to complete the exercise.

J. Paragraph Writing (Writing)

How is Yuko like you? How is she different from you? Write a paragraph with one of these titles: ***I Am Like Yuko***   *OR*

I Am Different from Yuko

_____

_____

_____

_____

_____

_____

_____

_____

_____

_____

_____

_____

_____

_____

_____

_____

_____

_____

_____

_____

_____

_____

UNIT ONE JOURNAL TOPIC SUGGESTIONS

Here are some journal topics for the theme of this unit. Choose any or all of them to write about in your journal. Be sure to read the section in the appendix on journal writing.

- My first day in this country
- It isn't easy being me
- One thing I wish I could change about myself
- One thing I would never change about myself
- How I want my children to be like me
- How I want my children to be different from me
- What I want to find out about X's (name of a classmate's country) culture
- What I know about X's (name of a classmate) culture
- A person in this class I would like to get to know better and why
- A person in this class who makes me feel uncomfortable and why

UNIT ONE VOCABULARY LOG

Write new vocabulary words here. Write a sentence for each word showing that you understand the meaning and can use the word correctly.

UNIT TWO

FAMILY AND RELATIONSHIPS

PART I — PREWRITING

Activity 1: Making Connections

Work in groups of four.

1. Each student in the group should choose one of the pictures and write as many words as possible about it for five minutes.
2. Look at each other's papers and try to find connections between them. Then look at the four pictures again. What connections can you find? Have one student in your group write down your ideas.
3. Put the list away. Each person in the group should find a partner in the class. Talk about the pictures. Discuss what your group said.

Activity 2: Freewriting

Freewriting is an exercise for your writing skills and thinking skills. The main idea in freewriting is to write as much as possible. Put your pen on the paper and don't pick it up. When you freewrite, you don't need to worry about spelling, grammar, or punctuation.

Your topic is "Family." For five minutes write as much as you can. Write everything that comes into your mind in English. Don't worry about mistakes. Don't edit. Use the space provided.

Next, in groups of four, read your writing to your classmates. (You don't need to show it to them.) You can stop to explain more if you want to. You should also ask each other questions.

Family

_____

_____

_____

_____

_____

_____

_____

_____

_____

_____

_____

_____

_____

_____

_____

_____

_____

_____

_____

_____

_____

_____

Activity 3: Identifying Family Members

In *Activity 1*, you started a story that connects
the pictures. Now think about your own family.
Write sentences about the members of your
family. First, write a sentence to explain what
relationship they are to you. Then, write another
sentence with additional information. Use the
example as a model.

EXAMPLE: John is my brother. He loves to play basketball.

Name and relationship	Additional information

PART II — STRUCTURE

Activity 1: Using Commas in a Series

Use commas to separate words or phrases that are in a series.

EXAMPLE: *I am taller than my mother, my father, and my uncle.*
I play tennis, swim, and write stories.
Do you come from Mexico, Guatemala, or El Salvador?

Something to remember: The comma before *and/or* is optional. The sentence can be written either way:
I am taller than my mother, my father, and my uncle.   OR
I am taller than my mother, my father and my uncle.

Notice that the comma comes immediately after the word or phrase. There is no space between the word and the following comma. There is one space after the comma.

> • = 1 space
> *Right:* I•am•taller•than•my•mother,•my•father,•and•my•uncle.
>
> *Wrong:* I•am•taller•than•my•mother•,•my•father•,•and•my•uncle.
>
> *Wrong:* I•am•taller•than•my•mother•,my•father•,and•my•uncle.
>
> *Wrong:* I•am•taller•than•my•mother,••my father,••and•my•uncle.

Notice that when the sentence has only two words or phrases, we usually don't use commas.

EXAMPLE: *I am taller than my mother or my father.*
I got up and took a shower.

Something more to remember: In a list, the pronoun *I* always comes last.
She is shorter than my mother, my father, and I.   NOT
She is shorter than I, my mother, and my father.

For the following sentences, decide whether to use commas to separate words. If you decide to use commas, then put them in the correct blank space.

EXAMPLE: José is a son_ _ a husband_ _ a father_ _ and a brother.
José is a son**,** a husband**,** a father**,** and a brother.

1. I have lived in a small village_ _ and a big city.

2. My mother hurt her leg_ _ her arm_ _ and her face in the accident.

3. Have you been to Dallas_ _ Pittsburgh_ _ or Chicago?

4. My sister plans to finish ESL classes_ _ _ get a nursing degree_ _ and help support our mother.

5. Squash_ _ spinach_ _ broccoli_ _ and brussel sprouts are not my kids' favorite vegetables, but I like them.

6. Tennis_ _ swimming_ _ and basketball are my sister's favorite activities.

7. My uncle can sing traditional folk songs_ _ or popular songs.

8. Julie_ _ Sara_ _ and Andrew are all under ten years old.

9. Think of all the Santa places in California. There's Santa Barbara_ _ Santa Clara_ _ Santa Cruz_ _ and Santa Ynez.

10. Do you have a large extended family_ _ or a small family?

Activity 2: Combining Sentences with Coordinating Conjunctions: *and, but, so,* and *or*

An easy way to combine sentences is to use the coordinating conjunctions *and, but, so,* and *or.** You have just practiced using these words for a series. You can also use them to combine sentences. For example:

| 1. S(ubject) + V(erb) + O(bject) *and* | 2. S(ubject) + V(erb) + O(bject) *but, so, or* |

My family speaks Spanish, **and** I speak Spanish, too. (and I do too/ and so do I)

My father speaks English, **but** my mother doesn't (speak English).

My mother stays home, **so** she doesn't have the opportunity to learn.

My brother may study here, **or** he may go to Los Angeles.

*Three other conjunctions: *for, nor,* and *yet* are a little formal and not as common as *and, but, so,* and *or.* We will not practice *for, nor,* and *yet* here, but you might want to review them in a grammar book.

In short sentences, the comma can be omitted.

A. In the sentences in the box above, underline each subject one time, and underline each verb two times.

These conjunctions all work the same way, but they have different meanings.

and = addition
but = contrast
so = result
or = choice

Don't forget to use a comma with these conjunctions when you are combining two independent clauses. (See page 33 for an explanation of **independent clauses**.)

Independent clauses

Coordinating conjunctions combine two **independent clauses**. An independent (main) clause has a subject and verb and is complete.

EXAMPLE:

Independent clause: *My grandfather speaks Turkish and Albanian.*
Independent clause: *I speak only Albanian.*

Two independent clauses connected with a coordinating conjunction: *My grandfather speaks Turkish and Albanian, but I only speak Albanian.*

In Unit 3 you will learn about **dependent clauses**.

SENTENCE COMBINING CHART: UNIT 2		
RELATIONSHIP	**INDEPENDENT AND INDEPENDENT CLAUSE**	**SAMPLE SENTENCES**
ADDITION	, and	I can sing well, **and** I can play the guitar like a professional.
CAUSE AND EFFECT	, so	It rained, **so** the picnic was cancelled.
CONTRAST	, but	I tried, **but** I couldn't do it.
CHOICE	, or	You can do it now, **or** I will do it later.

B. Write in the comma and the correct coordinator for the these sentences. There may be more than one correct answer.

EXAMPLE: My mother works hard, **but** she also has time for us.

1. My uncle is the president of a large company_____ he earns a lot of money.
2. My cousin is married_____ he has five children.
3. My sister is 26_____ she isn't married yet.
4. My great grandmother is 98 years old_____ she is still in very good health.
5. My brother-in-law has just arrived in the United States_____ he needs to learn English.
6. My husband works hard_____ he always has time to read to the children.
7. My boyfriend recently asked me to marry him_____ I haven't given him an answer yet.
8. She is living with her fiancé_____ her mother doesn't know.

C. Combine the following pairs of sentences with a coordinator. Write the new sentence, using the comma correctly.

EXAMPLE: I live in Seattle. My mother lives in New York.
   I live in Seattle, but my mother lives in New York.

1. My sister still lives in Guadalajara. My mother still lives in Guadalajara.

   _____

   _____

   _____

2. My uncle lives in the Ukraine. My aunt lives in San Diego.

   _____

   _____

3. My husband works two jobs. We can save a little money each month.

   _____

   _____

4. My son likes school. He doesn't like to do homework.

   _____

   _____

5. My aunt could earn money baby-sitting. She could learn English and get a higher paying job.

   _____

   _____

   _____

6. My grandparents were both musicians. I have no musical talent.

   _____

   _____

   _____

PART III — WRITING AND EDITING

Activity 1: Sentence Combining Editing

Look back at *Activity 3* in the *Prewriting* section. Write new sentences by combining as many sentences as possible, using *and, but, so,* and *or*.

EXAMPLE: My brother John, my uncle Joe, and I love to play basketball.
My brother John loves to play basketball, but my uncle Harry doesn't.

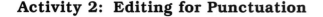

_____

_____

_____

_____

_____

_____

_____

_____

_____

Activity 2: Editing for Punctuation

Read this paragraph. Then read it again and add commas and periods where needed.

My Grandmother's Family

My grandmother is the most important person in our entire family so I always tell people that we are "Grandmother's Family" My grandfather died 20 years ago but Grandmother was already the boss in the family She had always managed the money made the important decisions and arranged the marriages My grandmother is strong but she is gentle too She listens to secrets and she always gives good advice I love admire and respect my grandmother I hope that my children grow up to be strong and honest like she is.

PART IV — WRITING AND REVISING ASSIGNMENT

Writing Assignment: My Family

Step 1: Reread the sentences you wrote for *Activity 1* in the *Writing and Editing* section. Which of your relatives has influenced you the most? How? Brainstorm and make notes about that person.

Step 2: Organize your notes by using one of the methods (chart, map, etc.) from Unit 1.

Step 3: Write a title and a topic sentence.

Step 4: Write the paragraph.

Revising Assignment: Peer Editing

Step 1: Exchange your paragraph with a partner. Read each other's stories.

Step 2: Is your partner's topic sentence clear? Are all of the sentences related to that topic? If not, tell your partner.

Step 3: On another piece of paper, write two or three questions about your partner's relative. Give the questions to your partner. Write the answers to the questions your partner wrote for you.

Step 4: Talk with your partner about how to add this new information to the paragraph.

Step 5: Rewrite your paragraph using some or all of the new information.

ADDITIONAL PRACTICE

A. Writing a Story (Writing)

Look at your notes for *Activity 1* in the *Prewriting* section. Write the story about the pictures.

_____

_____

_____

_____

_____

_____

_____

_____

_____

_____

_____

_____

_____

_____

_____

_____

_____

_____

_____

_____

_____

_____

_____

B. Relationship Vocabulary (Vocabulary)

What do you call the following people?

EXAMPLE: your mother's brother?   _____my uncle_____

1. your father's brother?   _____

2. your mother's mother?   _____

3. your mother's sister's son?   _____

4. your father's brother's daughter?   _____

5. your mother's sister?   _____

6. your father's mother and father?   _____

7. your father's father's father? _____

8. your sister's son? _____

9. your brother's son? _____

10. your sister's daughter? _____

11. your wife's (husband's) family? _____

12. your wife's (husband's) sister? _____

13. your father's new wife? _____

14. _____? _____
   (your question)

C. Talking about Family (Prewriting)

Find a picture of your family or someone
in your family. Prepare to talk about the
picture to your classmates in your next class.
After everyone talks, write notes to classmates
to ask for more information about their family.
Write the answers, and pass the notes back.

D. Writing about the Future (Writing)

Imagine that it is the year 2010. On a piece of paper, write eight sentences
about your family. Let your imagination run wild!

EXAMPLE: It is 2010. 1. I have four grandchildren.
2. My daughter is a doctor, my son is an architect, and the twins are famous movie stars.

The teacher will read the sentences, and the class can try to guess whose
family the sentences are about.

E. Identifying Subjects and Verbs (Structure)

Exchange the papers from Exercise C. Underline the subject(s)
of each sentence one time. Underline the verb(s) two times.

F. Combining Sentences with Coordinating Conjunctions (Editing)

The following sentences all have mistakes. Read them carefully. Write them again correctly.

EXAMPLE: 1. My cousin, and my uncle live in Boston.
My cousin and my uncle live in Boston.

1. My brother, my sister, my two cousins will immigrate to the United States next year.

   _____

   _____

2. My uncle Pedro could play the guitar very well, so he couldn't play the piano.

   _____

   _____

3. This summer vacation, I will visit my family, or will visit me.

   _____

   _____

4. My sister's fiancé has a good job, but they will buy a house.

   _____

   _____

5. My grandmother died a year ago, end my grandfather died soon after that.

   _____

   _____

6. All of my cousins, and my grandparents live in Texas.

_____

_____

7. My grandparents, and my parents, and my brothers all live in the same house.

_____

_____

8. I, my sister and my niece love the same kind of music.

_____

_____

9. My aunt loves living here, or my uncle doesn't.

_____

_____

10. Soon my parents will visit me, and will take them to visit the famous places.

_____

_____

G. Using Commas Correctly (Editing)

The following sentences have no commas. Read the sentences and add commas in the correct places.

1. My grandfather my father and my brother all have curly hair.
2. There are three Johns in the family but only one Joseph and one Michael.
3. Barbara Carole and Marilynn married and had children.
4. No one in the family lives in New Mexico Nevada or Texas.
5. I have three sisters-in-law three nephews and three nieces but only one mother-in-law.
6. My sister could give birth to twins triplets or quadruplets!

H. Editing a Story with Coordinating Conjunctions (Editing)

Read the story on the next page. On a separate piece of paper, rewrite the story and combine sentences when you see a relationship. You will need to change nouns to pronouns. Use *and, but, so,* and *or,* or other connectors. There are many different ways to do this correctly.

Juan's Dream

Juan Garza left his family in Durango. He took a bus to Texas. He was 19 years old. He was the third of six children. He had one hundred dollars in his pocket. Juan had a dream. He wanted to make money to send home to his family. He wanted to buy his mother a new house in Durango.

Juan found a job in a factory. He worked very hard. He worked long hours. Juan kept a picture of his family in his wallet. He looked at the picture whenever he felt homesick. He wanted to see his family. He didn't want to spend money on a ticket to Durango. Sometimes he wanted to quit his job. He didn't.

Juan began to study English. He got a better job. He started to save money. After three years, he had sent his mother a lot of money. His mother bought some land in the country. She started to build a new house for the family. Juan was happy.

Juan met a young woman from Texas. She didn't speak Spanish. They spoke in English. Juan was not homesick anymore. He began to have a new dream.

I. Writing Titles and Topic Sentences (Writing)

Read the following paragraph about Vu's family. Write a title and topic sentence to complete her paragraph.

_____

_____

We left our village at night so that nobody could see us. My mother was the only one who cried that night. After a dangerous journey, we arrived in a refugee camp in Thailand. We expected to stay there a short time, but we lived there for two years. I hated it there, but I never showed my feelings to my mother. Finally, we came to the United States. My father's brother and his family lived in Los Angeles. They were at the airport to meet us. We all cried when we got off the airplane, but those were tears of happiness.

UNIT TWO JOURNAL TOPIC SUGGESTIONS

Here are some journal topics for the theme of this unit. Choose any or all of them to write about in your journal. Be sure to read the section in the appendix on journal writing.

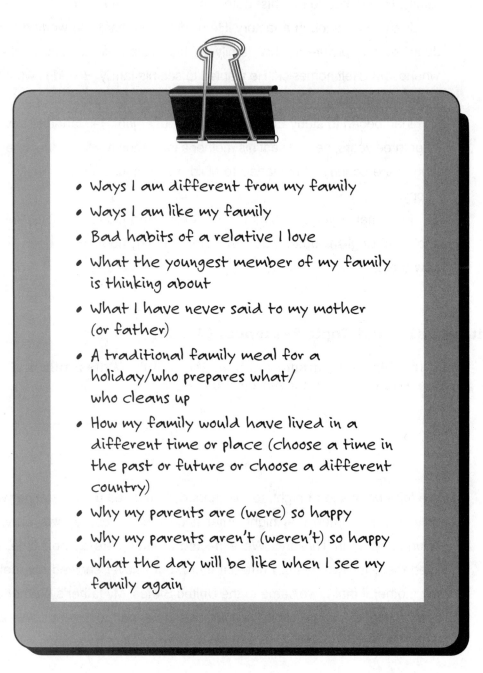

- Ways I am different from my family
- Ways I am like my family
- Bad habits of a relative I love
- What the youngest member of my family is thinking about
- What I have never said to my mother (or father)
- A traditional family meal for a holiday/who prepares what/ who cleans up
- How my family would have lived in a different time or place (choose a time in the past or future or choose a different country)
- Why my parents are (were) so happy
- Why my parents aren't (weren't) so happy
- What the day will be like when I see my family again

UNIT TWO VOCABULARY LOG

Write new vocabulary words here. Write a sentence for each word showing
that you understand the meaning and can use the word correctly.

UNIT THREE

EDUCATION

1. OJAI, CALIFORNIA pop 7,954

2. SHALLOW WATER, KANSAS pop. 94

3. NEW YORK, NEW YORK pop. 7,322,564

PART I — PREWRITING

Activity 1: Building an Argument

Look at the three schools. Decide which school you would like to send your son or daughter to. List your reasons below.

EXAMPLES OF REASONS: It is safe in the country.
There are more cultural opportunities in a big city.

(In the future,) I would like to send my son or daughter to _____

_____

Reasons:

1. _____

2. _____

3. _____

4. _____

5. _____

Find other students who made the same choice and form a group. Compare your lists of reasons.

As a whole class, write the reasons listed by each group on the board. Individuals from each group should be prepared to explain their reasons.

Activity 2: Group Writing Using Transitions

Working in the same groups as in *Activity 1*, decide which five ideas are the most important. Those are the five ideas your group will include in the paragraph.

Choose one person as the writer of the paragraph. Put the ideas in order. (Some writers put the most important reason first. Other writers put the most important idea last.) Don't forget to have an interesting title and a strong topic sentence to show your focus.

Use some of the following words to organize your writing.

First,	Third,	Finally,
First of all,	Fourth,	Another reason,
Second,	Next,	In conclusion,

Activity 3: Peer Editing

Exchange your group paragraph with another group. Read the new paragraph and discuss it in your group. If you have questions for the writers, write those questions after the paragraph. Also, write one comment telling what you like most about the paragraph.

EXAMPLES: Your ideas are very interesting. We especially like the last one because we didn't think of it.

OR

Your title was great. It made us want to read more.

Finally, read the questions and comments on your group paragraph and discuss them in your group.

PART II — STRUCTURE

Activity 1: Organizing by Location Using Prepositional Phrases

Look around your classroom. Notice where everything is. For example, maybe the teacher's desk is at the front of the room, or maybe it is not. Maybe the teacher's desk is at the side of the room. Is it on the right side or the left side? Write sentences to show where things are located in your classroom.

Here are some prepositions of location to help you.

at the front	to the right of	next to	across from
at the side	to the left of	near	in the back of
behind	below	on top of	

Write your sentences below.

_____

_____

_____

_____

_____

_____

_____

_____

_____

_____

_____

_____

_____

_____

Activity 2: Remembering Your Classroom

Think about your primary school. Think of yourself in the second grade, around 7 or 8 years old. Now close your eyes and imagine. In your mind, look at the walls. Notice what color they are. Is anything hung on them? Look out the windows of the room. What do you see there? Look at the ceiling and floor. Are there lights on the ceiling? Is the floor wooden or perhaps concrete? Are there desks, chairs, or benches? How many are there? How are they arranged in the room? Where does the teacher sit? Is there a big desk there? What's on the desk? Where is the blackboard? Is there anything written on it?

Draw your elementary school classroom in the space provided on the following page. Next, describe it to a partner. Start from the front of the room. Go around the room clockwise. Describe what is there. Don't forget to include the middle of the room.

Useful vocabulary

bench
bulletin board
chalkboard/blackboard
closet
flag
public address system

Describe the classroom again. This time, your partner will take notes about your classroom. After you finish, your partner should tell you about his or her classroom. You should take notes. From your notes, try to write a description of your partner's classroom.

Notes about _____'s classroom

_____

_____

_____

_____

_____

_____

_____

_____

_____

_____

Activity 3: Joining Sentences with Subordinating Conjunctions of Time

The following connecting words are used to join two sentences when there is a relationship of time between them. They are called subordinators.

after	*before*	*when*	*as soon as*
since	*while*	*whenever*	

A subordinator introduces a **dependent clause.** Like an **independent clause**, a **dependent clause** has a subject and verb, but it *depends* on an **independent clause** for complete meaning.

EXAMPLES:

We used to play baseball ***after*** school was over.
I had to make my bed ***before*** I went to school.
Everyone was quiet ***when*** the teacher entered the classroom.
Juan did his homework ***as soon as*** he got home.
I have been studying English ***since*** I was in seventh grade.*
Grigori was listening to the radio ***while*** he was studying for the test.
Ana used to chew gum ***whenever*** we had a test in class.

When a clause with these words begins a sentence (a **dependent clause**), you need to use a comma to separate it from the **independent clause**.

EXAMPLES:

After school was over, we used to play baseball.
Before I went to school, I had to make my bed.
When the teacher entered the classroom, everyone was quiet.
As soon as Juan got home, he did his homework.**
Since I was in seventh grade, I have been studying English.
While Grigori was studying for the test, he was listening to the radio.**
Whenever we had a test in class, Ana used to chew gum.

*When you use *since*, you need to use a present perfect tense in the independent clause.
**The noun always goes first and the pronoun second.

Combine the sentences using one of the subordinating time words. There may be more than one way to join each pair of sentences.

EXAMPLE: I was daydreaming. The teacher was explaining the assignment.
I was daydreaming while the teacher was explaining the assignment.

1. José listened to the radio. He was studying English.

   _____

   _____

2. Eduardo went to work (in the morning). He studied English (at night).

   _____

   _____

3. Kazu was 22 years old. He was accepted at City College.

   _____

   _____

4. Karl has been studying computers. He came here.

   _____

   _____

5. Svetlana studied a lot (last night). She took the test (this morning).

   _____

   _____

6. Yuri started an adult education class. He arrived in this city.

   _____

   _____

7. Maria calls her sister. She has problems in class.

   _____

   _____

8. Max had never used a computer. He took a writing class.

   _____

   _____

9. Miwako bought a sweatshirt in the bookstore. She was looking for her class text in the bookstore.

_____

_____

10. Kang Sun returned to Korea. She saved enough money for a ticket.

_____

_____

11. Rosalina hasn't been lonely in her classes. She started making friends.

_____

_____

12. Roberto has been teaching in the English as a Second Language Department. He got his master's degree.

_____

_____

Activity 4: Using Subordinating Conjunctions of Time

Think about your classmates and your teacher. Write ten sentences about them using time subordinators listed in *Activity 3*.

EXAMPLE: When the teacher called on Aurelio, he was reading a magazine.
Lin had never talked to me before we worked together in a group.

1. _____

   _____

2. _____

   _____

3. _____

   _____

4. _____

   _____

5. _____

   _____

6. _____

   _____

7. _____

   _____

8. _____

   _____

9. _____

   _____

10. _____

   _____

Activity 5: More Subordinating Conjunctions

There are other words that function the same way as the time words that you just practiced. Some of the most common **subordinating conjunctions** are *because, though, although* and *even though*. They too combine independent clauses and dependent clauses.

EXAMPLE: I was often late for school. I had to help my mother.

I was often late for school **because** I had to help my mother.

I did my best. I was very nervous.
I did my best **even though** I was very nervous.
I did my best **although** I was very nervous.

Use a comma when the clause begins the sentence.

EXAMPLE: *Because* I had to help my mother, I was often late for school.

SENTENCE COMBINING CHART: UNIT 3		
RELATIONSHIP	**INDEPENDENT AND INDEPENDENT CLAUSE**	**DEPENDENT AND INDEPENDENT CLAUSE**
ADDITION	, and	
CAUSE AND EFFECT	, so	because
CONTRAST	, but	although even though though
CHOICE	, or	
TIME		before • after as soon as since • when while • whenever

SENTENCE COMBINING CHART: EXAMPLE SENTENCES

RELATIONSHIP	INDEPENDENT AND INDEPENDENT CLAUSE	DEPENDENT AND INDEPENDENT CLAUSE
ADDITION	I can sing well, **and** I can play the guitar like a professional	
CAUSE AND EFFECT	It rained, **so** the picnic was cancelled.	**Because** it rained, the picnic was cancelled. The picnic was cancelled **because** it rained.
CONTRAST	I tried, **but** I couldn't understand.	**Although** I tried, I couldn't understand. I couldn't understand **even though** I tried.
CHOICE	You can do it now, **or** I will do it later.	
TIME		**When** he arrived, I left. I have been here **since** the room opened.

Combine the following sentences using *because, though, although,* or *even though*. Rewrite the examples with the dependent clause at the beginning.

EXAMPLE: Keiko cannot work off-campus. She has a student visa.

Keiko cannot work off-campus because she has a student visa.

Because Keiko has a student visa, she cannot work off-campus.

(Be sure to use the **noun first** and the **pronoun second**.)

1. I registered for only one class this semester. I have to work at night.

_____

_____

_____

_____

2. My sister can only take four units this semester. She can't afford more tuition.

_____

_____

_____

_____

3. Pedro passed the course. He failed the final exam.

_____

_____

_____

_____

4. Phillipe can't apply for financial assistance. He isn't a resident student.

_____

_____

_____

_____

5. Takahiro didn't get a scholarship. He had a high GPA.

_____

_____

_____

_____

6. Mai got a "C" on her paper. She rewrote it several times.

_____

_____

_____

_____

PART III — WRITING AND EDITING

Activity 1: Recognizing and Changing Sentence Fragments into Sentences

Sentence fragments are parts of sentences, but they are incomplete as sentences. Sentence fragments occur naturally and often in everyday conversation, but they are not common and they are not usually acceptable in writing.

> **EXAMPLE:** (Okay in conversation)   *A: Who're you going with?*
>   *B: My brother.* (fragment)

In writing, there are three common types of fragments.

1. Sentences without subjects

   EXAMPLE: Came to the United States three years ago.

2. Sentences without verbs

   EXAMPLE: New York, Chicago, and L.A.

3. Dependent clauses without independent clauses

   EXAMPLE: Because I wanted to find out about life in the United States.

Rewrite each of the three fragments in the box to make complete sentences. You will need to add some of your own words.

1. _____

   _____

2. _____

   _____

3. _____

   _____

Activity 2: Recognizing Fragments

Read the sentences on the next page. If a sentence is a fragment, write **F** next to the sentence. If a sentence is complete, write **CS** next to the sentence. Correct the fragments.

EXAMPLE: <u>F</u>   Because Genaro's paragraph was so interesting.

Everyone congratulated Genaro because his paragraph was so interesting.

1. _____ Because I am interested in painting, I'm enrolling in an art class.

   _____

   _____

2. _____ After I had gone to the bookstore.

   _____

   _____

3. _____ While he was standing on line in the Admissions Office, was filling out an application for financial assistance.

   _____

   _____

   _____

4. _____ You need to show your student ID when you check out a book.

   _____

   _____

5. _____ Even though Jorge has a degree from his own country.

   _____

   _____

6. _____ Last on line at the bookstore.

   _____

   _____

7. _____ Since my first semester here.

   _____

   _____

8. _____ Because the tuition is high.

   _____

   _____

Activity 3: Editing for Sentence Fragments

Read the story of Rosie Wang. On the next page, rewrite the paragraph by correcting the fragments. You will need to add coordinating conjunctions or subordinators. There is more than one way to rewrite and edit this paragraph.

A Busy Place

Life in Taipei, the capital of Taiwan, is busy. I live in Taipei, and I am busy every day. Because I have a lot of things to do. Wake up at 6 o'clock and study. Then dress, eat breakfast and ride my motor scooter to school. I attend Taipei National University. Best one in Taiwan. I have been studying there. Since last spring. My major business. Business people are the busiest of all Taiwanese. International trade is very important to Taiwan's economy so. Business people are always busy, working long hours. Because I like being busy. I don't mind working long hours. These days I study all day long. Part time job at night, four nights a week. I tutor middle school students in English, Chinese, and mathematics. My only day of rest is Sunday. When I go to the park with my boyfriend, Phillip Woo. I relax.

Rewrite the story of Rosie Wang here.

_____

_____

_____

_____

_____

_____

_____

_____

_____

_____

_____

_____

_____

_____

_____

PART IV — WRITING AND REVISING ASSIGNMENTS

Writing Assignment: My Best Teacher
My Worst Teacher

Step 1: **Thinking about the Topic and Brainstorming**

Think about the best teacher you've ever had. What grade were you in? What was the teacher's name? What did she or he teach? Why did you like this teacher?

Draw a picture of that wonderful person in the space provided on pages 61 and 62. (You don't have to be an artist.)

Write down as many adjectives as you can to describe this teacher. Then write a detail or example to illustrate each adjective.

Step 2: Get in groups of four or five students. Show your drawing and talk about your favorite teacher. Talk about your answers to the questions in *Step 1.* Read each adjective you wrote and your explanation.

Step 3: Now think of the worst teacher you've ever had. What grade were you in? What was the teacher's name? What did she or he teach? Why did you dislike this teacher?

Draw a picture of that person in the space provided on page 62. (You don't have to be an artist.)

Write down as many adjectives as you can to describe this teacher. Then write a detail or example to illustrate each adjective.

Step 4: Get back in your group and talk about your worst teacher. Show your drawing and talk about your answers to the questions in *Step 3.* Read each adjective you wrote and your explanation.

Step 5: Choose either your best teacher or your worst teacher. Write a paragraph about that person. Include a strong topic sentence and your examples to support it. Don't forget an interesting title. Remember to stay focused.

My Best Teacher

_____
(name)

_____
(grade/subject)

a. _____
(adjective)

_____
(example or explanation)

b. _____
(adjective)

_____
(example or explanation)

c. _____
(adjective)

_____
(example or explanation)

My Worst Teacher

_____
(name)

_____
(grade/subject)

a. _____
(adjective)

_____
(example or explanation)

b. _____
(adjective)

_____
(example or explanation)

c. _____
(adjective)

_____
(example or explanation)

Revising Assignment

Read your paragraph carefully. Then, answer these questions about it.

1. Is the topic sentence clear and interesting?

   Yes _____   No _____   It could be better. _____

2. Do you use more than one adjective to describe your teacher?

   Yes _____   I could add more. _____

3. Do you have an example to explain each adjective?

   Yes _____   I need to add explanations. _____

4. Are all of the sentences related to your main idea?

   Yes _____   I need to cut. _____

5. Do you have a good concluding sentence?

   Yes _____   Not yet. _____

If all of your answers are *yes*, you can submit your paper. If not, make improvements, and then submit your paper.

ADDITIONAL PRACTICE

A. Prepositions of Location (Structure)

Look at the three schools pictured at the beginning of this unit. Write ten sentences using *there is / there are* about the pictures. Use a prepositional phrase in each sentence.

EXAMPLE: There is a flag pole <u>in front of the school.</u>

PREPOSITIONS OF LOCATION			
next to	near	in front of	in back of
behind	across from	under	on top of
over	between	on the side of	in the middle of
by	on	in	

1. _____

2. _____

3. _____

4. _____

5. _____

6. _____

7. _____

8. _____

9. _____

10. _____

B. Prepositions of Location (Structure/Vocabulary)

Use a map of your campus, or use the map provided here. Answer the questions in complete sentences.

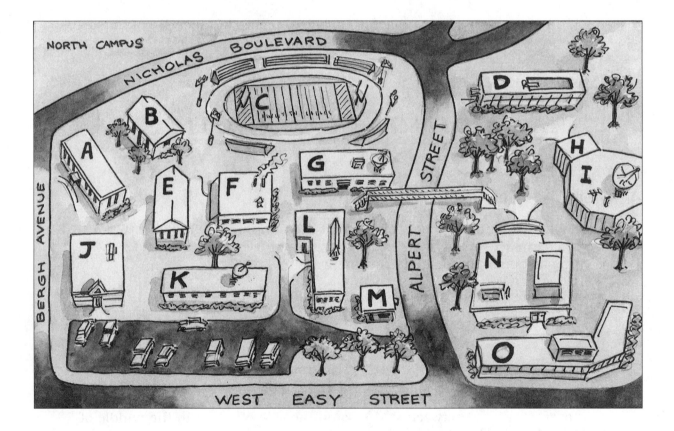

A ESL Building	**H** Technology Center	**N** Theater
B Foreign Languages Building	**I** Science Complex	**O** Student Services and
C Track/Football Field	**J** Bookstore	Administration
D Gymnasium/Indoor Pool	**K** Computer Lab	(Nurse's Office, Security,
E Business Studies Building	**L** Admissions and Records	President's Office,
F Cafeteria	**M** Counseling Center/	Personnel, Student Lounge,
G Library	Financial Aid	& Study Area, Career Center)

1. In what building is the Admissions Office located?

   _____

   _____

2. Where is the Student Services Building?

   _____

   _____

3. Where can students eat on campus? (Answer with name and location.)

   _____

   _____

4. Where is the ESL office located?

   _____

   _____

5. Where can students use computers?

   _____

   _____

6. Where can students get help selecting classes?

   _____

   _____

7. Where can resident students apply for financial assistance?

   _____

   _____

8. Where can students find out about careers and temporary jobs? Where is that office?

   _____

   _____

9. Where can students go if they feel sick?

   _____

   _____

10. Where can students receive advice about what to study?

   _____

   _____

C. Freewriting (Prewriting)

In five minutes, write as much as you can about the topic, "My Educational Goals." Remember when freewriting to write as much and as quickly as you can. Don't worry about mistakes.

D. Identifying Dependent and Independent Clauses (Structure)

Read each of the following sentences carefully. Underline the dependent clause one time. Underline the independent clause two times.

EXAMPLE: <u>Because I work during the day</u>, <u><u>I have to study at night.</u></u>

1. I like to do homework, and I know that it is important.

2. I like to do homework because it helps me study.

3. As soon as he arrived in the classroom, he put his homework on the desk.

4. I couldn't do my homework last night even though I wanted to.

5. She was my favorite teacher, but I never told her.

6. This semester I bought a new dictionary, a notebook, and three textbooks.

7. I try to read whenever I have a little free time.

8. He has been speaking only in English since he arrived here last month.

9. Although he was a very strict teacher, he was well liked.

10. You shouldn't give up when a course is difficult.

E. Editing Sentence Fragments (Structure/Editing)

Rewrite the following sentence fragments to make complete sentences.

1. After I finish a difficult exam.

   _____

   _____

2. Before I came to this country.

   _____

   _____

3. When I finish ESL classes.

_____

_____

4. As soon as I get my certificate or degree.

_____

_____

5. Since I started this class.

_____

_____

6. Whenever I use a computer.

_____

_____

7. While I'm a student at this college.

_____

_____

8. Because I didn't do the last homework assignment.

_____

_____

9. Although I haven't mastered English yet.

_____

_____

10. Even though I have often tried.

_____

_____

F. Academic Vocabulary (Vocabulary)

It's important to know these terms when planning your future. Match
the following vocabulary items with the best definition.

1. enroll

2. transfer

3. AA or AS degree
   (Associate of Arts/
   Associate of Science)

4. BA or BS degree
   (Bachelor of Arts/
   Bachelor of Science)

5. certificate

6. major

7. required course

8. career

9. due date

10. credits; units

11. GPA* (grade point average)

12. high school diploma

13. scholarship

a. the last day to hand in an
   assignment or paper

b. an official paper showing that
   course work in an area is complete

c. *to register* for a course or class

d. a certification of study received after
   completing high school requirements

e. average of all grades for one semester

f. a course that you must take before
   another course; a *prerequisite*

g. a certification of study given by
   a 4-year college or university

h. a field of employment; a *profession*

i. a certification of study given by
   a 2-year college

j. a unit of counting course work in
   an educational institution

k. money awarded for study

l. to continue studying at another
   educational institution

m. a specialization of study

*How to calculate your GPA: It is the average of all of your grades for
one semester. This is how most schools in the United States calculate GPA.

A = 4 points   B = 3 points   C = 2 points   D = 1 point   F = 0 points

Example: Reading   B   (3 points)
Writing   A   (4 points)
Grammar   C   (2 points)
Spanish   D   (1 point)
Total 10 points divided by 4 courses = 2.5 GPA

What was your GPA last semester? _____

If you are a continuing student, what is your CPA (cumulative grade
point average)? _____

G. Writing a Paragraph of Description (Writing)

Think of a title, an introductory sentence, and a concluding sentence
for the paragraph you wrote with your group in *Activity 2* in the *Prewriting*
section about the kind of school where your children would get the best
education. Rewrite the paragraph, including the title, introduction,
and conclusion.

H. Writing Descriptive Sentences (Prewriting/Writing)

Sit somewhere on campus and draw a picture of what you see. Take only ten minutes to do this. In class, join a group. Describe what you drew to your group. Each person should take a turn speaking. The group can ask you questions about your picture. Finally, the group should choose ten sentences to describe the campus, and write them below.

1. _____

_____

2. _____

_____

3. _____

_____

4. _____

_____

5. _____

_____

6. _____

_____

7. _____

_____

8. _____

_____

9. _____

_____

10. _____

_____

I. Informal Letter Writing/Giving Advice (Writing)

Read the story about Quan Le. Write a short letter to her on the following page. Can you sympathize with her? Can you give her advice?

A Different Way

I am a good student, but I don't like to talk a lot in class. In my country, students don't talk a lot in class. They listen to what the teacher says, and they write it down. Sometimes, the teacher asks students to recite from memory. That is how I learned in the past. I memorized things. However, I can't memorize English conversation. I know that I need to speak English, but I'm not used to speaking.

I get good grades on all my tests here. I am good in grammar because I memorize all the rules. I know the rules just as well as the teacher knows them. In reading class, I read and reread the stories. I underline new vocabulary. I look up new words in my English-Vietnamese dictionary. I know how to find the answer to reading questions. In spite of this, I can't discuss the readings very well. I want to discuss them, but by the time I think of what I want to say, it's too late.

I need to study English a different way. My friend, Tran, speaks English well. She spends a lot of time talking to people. She has a job as a waitress in a Japanese restaurant. Her boyfriend is Japanese. They speak English to one another. I need to find someone to whom I can speak English. I need to talk in class. But it's very hard for me. I feel so alone. I wish someone could tell me what to do. I really want to speak English well.

_____
(your street address)

_____
(your city, state)

_____
(date)

Dear Quan Le,

_____

_____

_____

_____

_____

_____

_____

_____

_____

_____

_____

_____

_____

_____

_____

_____

_____

Sincerely,

_____
(your name)

UNIT THREE JOURNAL TOPIC SUGGESTIONS

Here are some journal topics for the theme of this unit. Choose any or all of them to write about in your journal.

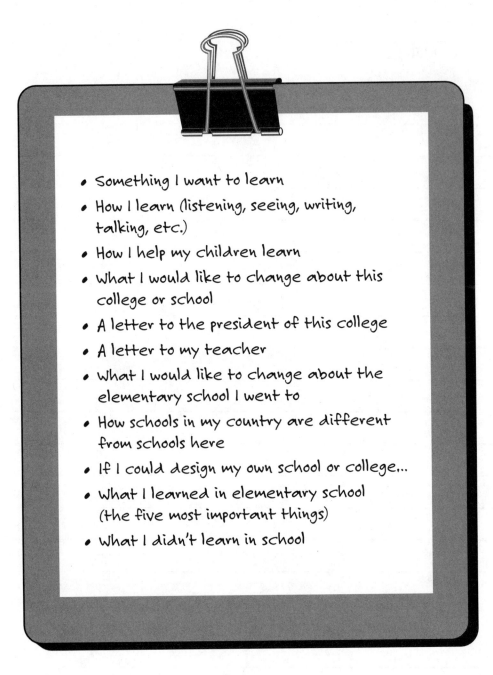

- Something I want to learn
- How I learn (listening, seeing, writing, talking, etc.)
- How I help my children learn
- What I would like to change about this college or school
- A letter to the president of this college
- A letter to my teacher
- What I would like to change about the elementary school I went to
- How schools in my country are different from schools here
- If I could design my own school or college...
- What I learned in elementary school (the five most important things)
- What I didn't learn in school

UNIT THREE VOCABULARY LOG

Write new vocabulary words here. Write a sentence for each word showing
that you understand the meaning and can use the word correctly.

_____

_____

_____

_____

_____

_____

_____

_____

_____

_____

_____

_____

_____

_____

_____

_____

_____

_____

_____

_____

_____

_____

UNIT FOUR

WORK

PART I — PREWRITING

Activity 1: Discussing the Picture

Look at the picture with a partner. Decide what jobs the people are doing. Discuss what training is needed to do the job. Talk about the good and bad points of this kind of work.

Activity 2: Discussing Your Job

Now think about the job you do or one you did in the past. If you have never worked, think about a job you are familiar with. Use the chart to brainstorm the good and bad things about your job. Then talk to a classmate about it.

Job: _____

Good Things about My Job	Bad Things about My Job

Activity 3: Brainstorming/Vocabulary

How many job titles do you know? In groups of three students, make an alphabetical list with one job title for each letter. Work quickly! You only have five minutes.

When you finish, the class can make a master list for the board. Each group gets 1 point for a correct answer and 2 points if the answer is also original. Good luck.

EXAMPLE: **A** architect _____

A _____   N _____

B _____   O _____

C _____   P _____

D _____   Q _____

E _____   R _____

F _____   S _____

G _____   T _____

H _____   U _____

I _____   V _____

J _____   W _____

K _____   X _____

L _____   Y _____

M _____   Z _____

Activity 4: Expressing Relationships

Discuss the relationship among the words in each group below.

1. pencil
    typewriter
    computer

2. machete
    lawnmower
    tractor

3. aspirin
    antibiotics
    home remedy

4. muscle
    machine
    robot

5. office
    field
    classroom

6. rice planting
    house painting
    mural painting

Write a sentence for each group of words. You do not need to use all three words in one sentence.

EXAMPLE: A pencil is cheaper than a typewriter.   OR

Learning to use a computer takes a lot of time.

1. _____

2. _____

3. _____

4. _____

5. _____

6. _____

Activity 5: Vocabulary

Look at the pictures. Label the tool(s) in each picture, and write the name of the occupation(s) each is used for. Then add some drawings of your own and have another student write the label and occupation.

Activity 6: Freewriting

Your topic is "My Future Career Plans." For five minutes write as much as you can. Write everything that comes into your mind in English. Don't worry about mistakes. Don't edit.

Then, in groups of four students, exchange papers with your classmates. Keep exchanging until everyone in the group has read everyone else's paper. After reading, talk about the similarities and differences of your plans. Talk about how you will accomplish your career goals.

_____

_____

_____

_____

_____

_____

_____

_____

_____

_____

_____

_____

_____

_____

_____

_____

_____

_____

_____

PART II — STRUCTURE

Activity 1: Connecting Sentences with Transitions: *therefore* and *however*

The transitions *therefore* and *however* are used to join two sentences when there is a relationship between them of result or reason *(therefore)*, or contrast *(however)*. They are used in writing that has a formal style, such as an academic essay, a textbook passage, a newspaper or magazine article, a business letter or a government document. Their everyday equivalents are:

>   *therefore = so*   *however = but*

Some other words that can be used as transitions are *thus, as a result, consequently,* and *hence* for *therefore*; and *nevertheless* for *however.*

1. When these words join two sentences, they usually occur between the two sentences (two independent clauses) and are followed by a semicolon (;).

    EXAMPLES: a. Un Taek's work involves a lot of traveling; **therefore,** he is out of town about half the year.

    b. Maria's job doesn't pay well; **however,** her boss treats her very well.

2. These example sentences can also be pairs of sentences with the joining words at the beginning of the second sentence of each pair.

    a. Un Taek's work involves a lot of traveling. **Therefore,** he is out of town about half the year.

    b. Maria's job doesn't pay well. **However,** her boss treats her very well.

SENTENCE COMBINING CHART: UNIT 4

RELATIONSHIP	INDEPENDENT AND INDEPENDENT CLAUSE	DEPENDENT AND INDEPENDENT CLAUSE	INDEPENDENT AND INDEPENDENT CLAUSE
ADDITION	, and		
CAUSE AND EFFECT	, so	because	; therefore,
CONTRAST	, but	although even though though	; however,
CHOICE	, or		
TIME		before • after as soon as since • when while • whenever	'

SENTENCE COMBINING CHART: EXAMPLE SENTENCES

RELATIONSHIP	INDEPENDENT AND INDEPENDENT CLAUSE	DEPENDENT AND INDEPENDENT CLAUSE	INDEPENDENT AND INDEPENDENT CLAUSE
ADDITION	I can sing well, **and** I can play the guitar like a professional.		
CAUSE AND EFFECT	It rained, **so** the picnic was cancelled.	**Because** it rained, the picnic was cancelled. The picnic was cancelled **because** it rained.	It rained; **therefore,** the picnic was cancelled. It rained. **Therefore,** the picnic was cancelled.
CONTRAST	I tried, **but** I couldn't understand.	**Although** I tried, I couldn't understand. I couldn't understand **even though** I tried.	I tried; **however,** I couldn't understand. I tried. **However,** I couldn't understand.
CHOICE	You can do it now, **or** I will do it later.		
TIME		**When** he arrived, I left. I have been here **since** the room opened.	

Combine the pairs of sentences into one sentence using *therefore* or *however*.

EXAMPLE: I need a job that doesn't require lifting heavy objects. I can't work for a moving company.

I need a job that doesn't require lifting heavy objects; therefore, I can't work for a moving company.

1. Serafin wants to be a civil engineer. He is looking for an internship with an engineering company for the summer.

   _____

   _____

2. Thuan would like to go back to school to study business. He doesn't have enough money to pay for his tuition.

   _____

   _____

3. No one likes to clean out bathrooms. Some janitors have to do it.

   _____

   _____

4. Business people can make quite a lot of money. Many of them have to work long hours for it.

   _____

   _____

5. Claudine is a cashier. She wants to be an artist.

   _____

   _____

6. Chizuko wants to travel. She would like to be a flight attendant.

   _____

   _____

7. Tomas had no idea how to serve dinner. He had a lot of problems his first day as a waiter.

   _____

8. Susana often feels upset. She never lets her customers know it.

   _____

   _____

Activity 2: Practice with *so* and *but*

Write down the names of five people you know who are working. With a partner, discuss each person. Describe what they do at their jobs. Use *so* and *but* to talk about the person and his or her job.

EXAMPLE: Sergio – "Sergio is a busboy. He carries trays, sets tables, and clears tables, but he doesn't serve food. Oh, he pours water, too."

Activity 3: From Spoken to Written English

Now, write five of the sentences you have spoken in *Activity 2*. Decide whether to use *so/therefore*, or *but/however* in each sentence.

1. _____

   _____

2. _____

   _____

3. _____

   _____

4. _____

   _____

5. _____

   _____

Activity 4: Recognizing Run-on Sentences

Run-on sentences are two or more sentences (independent clauses) written together without proper connecting words or punctuation.

EXAMPLE RUN-ON SENTENCE: I like my job my manager is very fair.

One way to correct a run-on sentence is by simply adding punctuation to separate the independent clauses.

EXAMPLE: *I like my job. My manager is very fair.*

Another way to correct a run-on sentence is by adding connecting words such as coordinating conjunctions, subordinators, or transitions.

EXAMPLE: *I like my job because my manager is very fair.*

In this example, it is better to add a connecting word because it clarifies meaning.

Read these sentences. Write **RO** next to the run-on sentences. Write **CS** next to the complete sentences. Rewrite the run-on sentences correctly.

1. _____ Lilia works long hours she gets very tired.

   _____

   _____

2. _____ My uncle manages a successful photocopy business.

   _____

   _____

3. _____ I like to work with numbers I plan to work in a bank some day.

   _____

   _____

4. _____ My job is hard it is boring too.

   _____

   _____

5. _____ Sam sets tables, pours water, then he clears the tables.

   _____

   _____

6. _____ Babysitters have a lot of responsibility, but they receive little pay.

   _____

   _____

7. _____ Tania knows how to use a computer for word processing now
   she wants to learn how to use a spreadsheet.

   _____

   _____

8. _____ Men often earn more than women for doing the same jobs.

   _____

   _____

PART III — WRITING AND EDITING

Activity 1: Interview Research

In *Activity 6* of the *Prewriting* section you wrote about your career plans. Like most students, you probably have questions about how you can reach your goal. There are many places to get answers to these questions. Write down two that you can think of, and then compare your answers with the rest of the class.

My ideas:

_____   _____

Other ideas:

_____

_____

Write some questions that you would like to ask about reaching your career goals. Choose the best place(s) from the list above, then go and find the answers.

EXAMPLE: Do I need a certificate, an AA degree, or a BA degree to become a kindergarten teacher in the United States?

_____

_____

_____

_____

_____

_____

_____

_____

_____

_____

_____

Activity 2: Editing Questions and Answers

Exchange your questions and answers from *Activity 1* with a partner.
Read each other's questions and answers. You are going to prepare a short
guide for students interested in your career. Write a paragraph that gives
useful information.

Career: _____

Useful information:

_____

_____

_____

_____

_____

_____

_____

_____

_____

_____

_____

_____

_____

_____

_____

_____

_____

_____

_____

_____

_____

PART IV — WRITING AND REVISING ASSIGNMENT

Writing Assignment: Job Search

Step 1: In groups of four or five students form a *company*. Decide what kind of company you are. Invent a name. Choose a president or CEO (Chief Executive Officer), vice president, receptionist, and one or two directors of personnel. Decide on a job that you would like to hire someone to do.

Step 2: Use the outline on page 89. Write down the job title. Brainstorm the qualifications you want applicants to have. Brainstorm the job responsibilities. How much is the salary? What are the benefits?

Step 3: Look at some job announcements in a newspaper. (Also, see the sample on page 92). Notice the kind of information that is given. Add to your outline on page 89. Write a job announcement for the job for your company. It will be more interesting if you add a logo or picture. Edit it. Does it include all of the important information? Is it clear and correct?

Step 4: Post the job announcements in the classroom.

Step 5: Now imagine that you are an individual outside of your company. You are looking for a job. Choose one of the jobs posted and write a letter of application. You can follow the sample on page 93.

Step 6: Go back into your companies and read your mail. Underline all of the sentences in the letter that show the applicant's qualifications. Choose two or three applicants to interview for your job. Announce your choices.

Step 7: Look at the sample interview questions on page 90. Use the space on that page to write eight interview questions for your job vacancy. Decide who will ask which question.

Step 8: Interview your applicants. You can do this in groups, or the whole class can observe each group interview. Then, have a short company meeting to decide who to hire. Announce whom you have hired and why.

Note to teachers: This assignment will take several class sessions to complete.

COMPANY OUTLINE

Company Name: _____

President or CEO: _____

Vice President: _____

Director (s) of Personnel:_____

Receptionist: _____

We need to hire a _____ (job title)

Job Responsibilities: _____

_____

_____

_____

_____

_____

Skills/Education Required: _____

_____

_____

_____

Salary or Hourly Wage:_____

Benefits: _____

_____

_____

_____

_____

Sample Interview Questions

What are your strong points (strengths)?
What are your weak points (weaknesses)?
Why do you want this job?
Why do you want to work for this company?
How are you qualified for this job?
Why did you leave your last job?
Explain one difficulty in life that you have overcome?
What would you do if you saw a fellow employee stealing?

The following questions **cannot** be asked during a job interview in the United States.

What is your religion?
Have you ever been arrested?
Are you married?
Do you have children? Do you plan to have children?

Company Interview Questions

1. _____

   Who will ask the question? _____

2. _____

   Who will ask the question? _____

3. _____

   Who will ask the question? _____

4. _____

   Who will ask the question? _____

5. _____

   Who will ask the question? _____

6. _____

   Who will ask the question? _____

7. _____

   Who will ask the question? _____

8. _____

   Who will ask the question? _____

Revising Assignment

See *Step 3* in the *Writing Assignment*.

After writing your job application letter (*Step 5*), have a classmate read it and answer these questions.

1. Are there three paragraphs?

   Yes _____   No _____

2. Does the first paragraph clearly explain the purpose of the letter?

   Yes _____   No _____

3. Does the second paragraph explain job qualifications for this job?

   Yes _____   No _____

4. Does the last paragraph explain when the applicant is available for an interview and how to contact him or her?

   Yes _____   No _____

5. Is the form and punctuation of the letter similar to the sample letter?

   Yes _____   No _____

6. Is the letter neat?

   Yes _____   No _____

7. Is the spelling correct?

   Yes _____   No _____

If the answer to any of these questions is *no*, write your letter again with revisions and corrections. Use the sample letter on page 93 as a guide, but do not copy it.

ADDITIONAL PRACTICE

A. Sample Advertisement and Job Application Letter (Prewriting)

Daily News
CLASSIFIED ADVERTISEMENTS

The Redmore Resort Hotel is looking for an energetic, creative individual with strong communication skills and extraordinary interpersonal skills to join our team. Experience coordinating weddings and conferences preferred, but will consider training a motivated, hardworking person.

Job description

Title: Events Coordinator (Full time, administrative)
Location: Honolulu
Salary: Negotiable
Benefits: * Full medical/dental coverage for employee
and dependents
  * Stock option
  * Retirement package
  * Two weeks paid vacation a year
  * Six paid sick days a year

Forward resume and letter of interest to: Janet Jordan, Director of Personnel, The Redmore Resort Hotel, 1000 Coast View Road, Honolulu, HI 96877

SAMPLE JOB APPLICATION LETTER

1551 Keeaumakaii Street
Honolulu, HI 96877
June 5, 1997

Janet Jordan
Director of Personnel
The Redmore Resort Hotel
1000 Coast View Road
Honolulu, HI 96877

Dear Ms. Jordan:

I would like to apply for the position of Special Events Coordinator that you advertised in the Sunday issue of the *Daily News.* I have long admired your world-famous resort, and I would like the opportunity to join such a first-class team.

You are looking for someone with energy, creativity, and extraordinary interpersonal skills. The letters of reference attached will show you that I am that person. I have recently completed a Hotel and Restaurant Culinary Program. As a result, I am experienced in all aspects of hotel management. In addition, I speak three languages fluently.

I feel that I have the qualifications, energy, and enthusiasm that you are looking for in a Special Events Coordinator. I am available for an interview at your convenience. I look forward to meeting you and introducing myself. You can call me at 503-966-5555 and leave a message.

Sincerely,

Claudia Vasquez

Claudia Vasquez

Answer the following questions about Claudia's letter.

1. What punctuation did Claudia use after the greeting?

   _____

2. What is the purpose of Claudia's first paragraph?

   _____

   _____

   _____

3. What is the purpose of Claudia's second paragraph?

   _____

   _____

   _____

4. What is the purpose of Claudia's third paragraph?

   _____

   _____

   _____

5. How did Claudia use the advertisement when writing her letter? Underline all of the words in the advertisement and in the letter that are the same.

6. Does Claudia have a lot of experience? _____ Did she say that in her letter? _____ What did she emphasize, experience or education? Why?

   _____

   _____

   _____

7. Would the style and form of this letter be the same in your country? How would it be different?

   _____

   _____

   _____

B. Identifying Sentences (Structure)

Read these sentences carefully. Some are fragments, some are run-on sentences and others are complete sentences. Mark each sentence **F** = fragment **RO** = run-on and **CS** = complete sentence. Correct the fragments and the run-on sentences.

EXAMPLE: _RO_ Miguel is looking for a second job he needs to earn more.

Miguel is looking for a second job because he needs to earn more.   OR
Miguel needs more money; therefore, he is looking for a second job.

1. _____ Irma wants to quit her job she's going to have a baby soon.

   _____

2. _____ Jorge is taking a math class because many jobs require basic math skills.

   _____

3. _____ Because Ismael knows how to use a word processor.

   _____

4. _____ Is a good major because there are many jobs in that field now.

   _____

5. _____ Bilingual people have more job opportunities in most cities those people earn more too.

   _____

6. _____ Early Childhood Education is a popular major among ESL students.

   _____

7. _____ The Hotel, Restaurant, and Culinary Program is excellent many students want to enroll.

   _____

8. _____ Ludmilla doesn't want to study accounting she wants to study marine biology.

   _____

C. Application Vocabulary (Vocabulary)

Read these adjectives. Which ones best describe you to a potential employer? Check each word that describes you and write one reason why it does.

EXAMPLE: __X__ dependable   I always complete my work.

____ calm under pressure   ____ good with details

____ creative   ____ hardworking

____ dependable   ____ organized

____ efficient   ____ prompt

____ friendly   ____ responsible

____ good with numbers   ____ skilled

                              ____ other: _____

_____

_____

_____

_____

_____

_____

Now look at these verbs. Which have you done or can do?

EXAMPLE: __X__ organized   I organized a soccer team in high school.

____ coordinated   ____ managed

____ created   ____ organized

____ led   ____ other: _____

_____

_____

_____

_____

_____

_____

D. Preparing for an Interview (Writing/Vocabulary)

During an interview, the interviewer may ask you to describe your strengths and weaknesses. This is difficult to do, especially when you must list your weaknesses. You have to say *something*, but you don't want to sound like a bad employee. You can say something like, "People say I am a workaholic." (The company may love to have such a hard worker!) Another possible response is, "My coworkers and friends say I am too serious about my work because I always talk about it when I am at home. I always try to think of ways to do my job better."

Of course, you should always tell the truth about yourself, but this is not the time to be shy or modest.

Prepare yourself for an interview. Write down two or three of your strengths and one weakness. Be sure to give examples and explanations if needed.

My strengths: _____

_____

_____

_____

_____

My weaknesses: _____

_____

_____

_____

_____

E. Story (Structure)

Read the story about Kim Tae Sam. In the blank spaces, write words that help to tell the story.

You can use these words: *and, but, so, or, however, because, therefore, when, after, before,* and *although.*

Moving Up the Ladder

Kim Tae Sam was born in a farming village in Chollado, South Korea. _____ he was small, he used to help his parents plant rice in the field. He was a good student, _____ his parents sent him to school in Kwangju, a large city. He would visit his parents' village on school vacations. The rest of the year he remained in the city to study. Tae Sam studied hard _____ did well on the entrance examination for university. He attended a university in Seoul, far from his family. He only visited them in summer. During winter break, he studied English at a language school in Seoul.

Tae Sam chose to study computer science. He knew that there were many opportunities in this field _____ it was a new field. Tae Sam graduated from the university. His parents made the trip to Seoul to attend the graduation. They had never been to Seoul before. They felt uncomfortable. _____ the graduation, they went straight home. Tae Sam stayed in Seoul to look for a job. He got a job with an American company _____ he could speak English and he knew computers well.

_____ he had worked two years in Seoul, the company sent him to New York to work in its headquarters there. Tae Sam was happy to have the chance to travel, _____ he was sad _____ he would be very far away from home. In New York, Tae Sam met a Korean-American woman, Oh Hae Ja. They fell in love. Hae Ja was a teacher, _____ her work was very important to her. Tae Sam loved her. _____ she was not really like women in Korea, _____ she spoke Korean well.

Tae Sam's company was not doing well. They told him he had to return to Korea within six months. He asked Hae Ja to go back with him. She would not go. _____ , Tae Sam quit the company. _____ he quit, he had to tell his parents that he would not return to Korea. They were very upset. Then he used his savings to buy a small convenience store. _____ he did that, he and Hae Ja made plans to marry. Tae Sam worked seven days a week, twenty hours a day in the store. One day Tae Sam realized that his life had changed. He was always tired, _____ he could not think of anything but his store. What had happened to his career?

F. Informal Letter Writing (Writing)

Imagine that you are Tae Sam. You have to write a letter to your parents in Korea to explain why you have decided to stay in the United States. Write the letter.

> _____
>
> _____
>
> August 1, 1997
>
> Dear Mother and Father,
>
> _____
> _____
> _____
> _____
> _____
> _____
> _____
> _____
> _____
> _____
> _____
> _____
> _____
> _____
> _____
> _____
> _____
> _____
>
> Love,
>
> Tae Sam

UNIT FOUR JOURNAL TOPIC SUGGESTIONS

Here are some journal topics for the theme of this unit. Choose any
or all of them to write about in your journal.

- My dream job
- The best job I ever had
- The worst job I ever had
- How I feel about my present job
- What's most important to me in a job
  (money, hours, job satisfaction, etc.)
- What makes a good boss
- The worst job a person could have
- The best job a person could have
- Does society reward people in different
  careers fairly? (teacher, doctor,
  athlete, garbage collector, etc.)
- A prestige career that really isn't

UNIT FOUR VOCABULARY LOG

Write new vocabulary words here. Write a sentence for each word showing
that you understand the meaning and can use the word correctly.

UNIT FIVE

LEISURE AND RECREATION

PART I — PREWRITING

Activity 1: Vocabulary Warm-Up

In the chart, write down the activities you see in the picture on the opposite page. In the box at the right of the chart, write *like* for the activities you like to do, and write *dislike* for the activities you don't like to do. Compare your list with a classmate by talking about it.

Activity	

Activity 2: Talking about Leisure Activities

In groups of four, take turns telling about the things you do in your free time. If you don't understand what activity a person is talking about, ask that person to explain it to you.

Next, interview one person in your group about the things that he or she likes to do during free time. Find out *when, how often, where,* and *with whom* your classmate does the activity. Write your questions in the space provided on the next page. Then ask your partner and write notes on his or her answers. The first question is done as an example.

What   What do you like to do in your free time?

_____

When _____

_____

How often _____

_____

Where _____

_____

With whom _____

_____

Activity 3: Freewriting

For five minutes, write as much as you can on the topic, "Vacation."

Next, in groups of four students, exchange your papers.

_____

_____

_____

_____

_____

_____

_____

_____

Activity 4: Sorting or Categorizing

When people have free time, they do many different things. They exercise
and do sports such as volleyball, soccer, and swimming. They relax with
a book or in front of the TV. They work in the garden, do little things
around the house, and work on their cars. They visit friends, go out to
dinner, and go for hikes in the mountains. Some people even use
their free time to help others by volunteering at hospitals, senior citizen
centers, and homeless shelters.

Below you will find the activities of one of the authors, Lou. They are not sorted; that is, they are not put into categories that are similar. Your job is to rewrite the activities into groups which are similar in some way; for example, you might have a group of activities that require a lot of energy and cause a person to get tired after doing them. You might have another group of activities that someone would do with friends. There are many different ways to categorize. The way you organize is up to you. You *do not* need to include all the activities.

Lou's List of Free Time Activities

play bass with Jeff, my guitarist friend

listen to my CDs

practice classical guitar

swim for an hour every day at twelve noon

play tennis when I can with Pablo and John

water and weed the vegetable garden

do some creative writing at least once a week

read the *New Yorker* every week

go for a bike ride

walk my dog Lucy every morning

play basketball with Johnny after school

rent a video occasionally

listen to the radio every morning and evening

read about teaching

read novels, poems, and short stories

go for coffee with Frank once or twice a week

go to a movie

attend a concert once in a while

watch sports on TV every day

You can organize your categories for Lou's activities here. **Be sure to give each category a title.** Make 2, 3, or 4 categories.

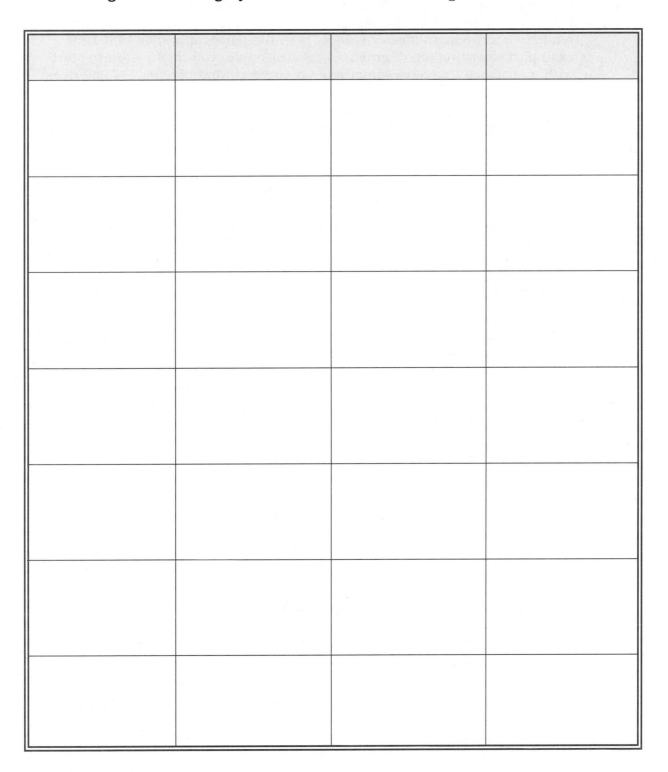

Activity 5: Writing a First Draft

Now, write a paragraph for each group of Lou's activities in *Activity 4*. Remember to introduce the paragraph with a topic sentence that tells the reader what the main idea or subject is in the paragraph. (See *Unit 1* for examples of writing topic sentences.) For example, you might want to start with a sentence that says something about what kind of activities Lou does and how often he does them.

EXAMPLE: Lou likes sports and plays them quite often.

_____

_____

_____

_____

_____

_____

_____

_____

_____

_____

_____

_____

_____

_____

_____

_____

_____

_____

_____

PART II — STRUCTURE

Activity 1: Writing Transition Sentences

Now that you have written paragraphs about Lou's activities, read them again. Answer these questions about them.

1. Do they seem to go well together, or do they need something to make them fit more closely together?

   _____

2. Does paragraph one lead the reader easily to paragraph two, or do you need a **transition sentence?** A **transition sentence** is one which moves the reader from one idea group to another group (one paragraph to another) by making a connection between the groups.

   EXAMPLE: *Lou likes sports a lot, but he also likes music.*

Notice that a transition sentence usually gives you an idea of what the next paragraph topic will be. In the case above, it is music. One other thing to notice is that writers often use the same sentence to change topics and to introduce a new topic. **This means that the topic sentence and the transition sentence can be the same.**

Now, read the paragraphs you wrote for *Activity 5* in the *Prewriting* section. If you do not have transition sentences, add them. Underline your transition sentences. Then, exchange your paper with a partner.

Were your paragraphs similar or different? _____

Are the transition sentences clear and helpful to you, the reader? _____

Activity 2: Using *such as, for example,* and *for instance*

Giving examples when you write makes your writing clearer and more interesting.

Such as, for example, and *for instance* are phrases that introduce examples. Notice the punctuation in these example sentences.

> There are many warm weather sports **such as** swimming, beach volleyball, and water skiing.

> There are many warm weather sports, **for example,** swimming, beach volleyball, and water skiing.

> There are many warm weather sports, **for instance,** swimming, beach volleyball, and water skiing.

For example and *for instance* need commas. *Such as* does not require punctuation.

Complete the following sentences. Try to give at least two examples for each sentence.

EXAMPLE: There are many ways to spend a Friday night such as dancing, going out with friends, or watching TV.

1. There are many team sports such as _____
   _____

2. There are many things to do on a Sunday morning such as _____
   _____

3. There are many popular individual sports such as _____
   _____

4. There are many places to sleep on a vacation such as _____
   _____

5. I like to do many activities on a day off, for example, _____
   _____

6. I like many kinds of music, for example, _____
   _____

7. I like different kinds of movies, for instance, _____
   _____

8. My friend has visited many interesting places, for instance, _____
   _____

PART III — WRITING AND EDITING

Activity 1: Writing with *such as, for example,* and *for instance*

Write your own sentences with *such as, for example,* and *for instance.*
Your sentences should relate to the interview you had with your partner
in *Activity 2* in the *Prewriting* section.

_____

_____

_____

_____

_____

_____

_____

_____

_____

_____

_____

_____

_____

_____

_____

_____

_____

_____

_____

_____

_____

_____

Activity 2: Editing Sentence Fragments with *such as,* *for example,* and *for instance*

Be careful when you use *such as, for example,* and *for instance.* Although it is possible to start a sentence with these words, students often make the mistake of writing sentence fragments by not adding a subject and verb.

EXAMPLES: Correct: For example, *you can swim, dive, or water ski.*

Incorrect: For example, swimming, diving, or water skiing. (no subject, no verb)

Correct: *You can do* many things at the beach, for example, swimming, diving, or water skiing.

Correct: *You can do* many things at the beach; for example, *you can swim, dive, or water-ski.*

In the last example there are two independent clauses. A semicolon connects the two sentences.

Read the following sentences. Write **CS** if the sentences are correct. Write **F** if a sentence is a fragment.

1. _____ Such as adventure stories, love stories and mysteries.

2. _____ For example, I like to go camping with my friends.

3. _____ For instance, dancing and going to concerts.

4. _____ He plays several sports well, for example, soccer, basketball, and volleyball.

5. _____ For example, you can walk, run, or work-out.

6. _____ For instance, sewing and knitting.

7. _____ He collects many things such as stamps and bottle caps.

8. _____ For instance, you can take the train.

9. _____ To live on a tropical island such as Hawaii or Tahiti.

10. _____ Mountains like Mt. Everest, for instance.

Activity 3: Writing Sentences with *such as, for example,* and *for instance*

A. For each category, write down notes about your personal preferences.

Outdoor Sports	Indoor Activities	Music	Books	TV Programs

B. Now, write a sentence for each category, using *such as, for example,* or *for instance.*

1. _____

_____

2. _____

_____

3. _____

_____

4. _____

_____

5. _____

_____

Activity 4: Form of an Essay

To understand the structure of an essay, it is helpful to analyze one. Read this essay and answer the questions that follow it.

Me and My Guitars

Everyone has a hobby, something they like to do whenever they can. My hobby is the guitar. I'm not the greatest player in the world, but I have eventually become good enough to entertain myself, my family, and my friends. I have also made a little money playing in clubs and for parties and weddings. I have been playing for over 30 years. Over that time, I have owned several guitars. Each one was special to me, and each one brought a different kind of music to me.

I can remember my first guitar quite well. It was a cheap Harmony steel string guitar that hurt my fingers when I played it for more than ten minutes. Despite the pain that Harmony gave me, it gave me a lot of pleasure. When I learned a new song on the guitar, I would rush out to my friends to play it for them. Then the Beatles came to the United States. After seeing the Beatles, I decided my scratchy-sounding Harmony wasn't good enough. I wanted an electric guitar. I wanted to be like the Beatles. Of course, I still wasn't a very good guitar player, and I could hardly read music. However, I begged my parents to buy me an electric guitar. One Saturday, my father took me to a music store and bought one for me.

Ah, my first electric! It was a Gibson ES355, sunburst with double cutaways. What an instrument! It had two volume controls, two tone controls, and a position switch that gave different sounds. That Gibson changed things for me because I had to promise my parents to take guitar lessons. I took lessons for about two years altogether. My teachers were jazz guitarists. That caused a problem for me. When it came time to form a rock group, which every young guy with a guitar wanted to do after he'd seen the Beatles, I was given the honor of being lead guitarist. At that time, in imitation of the Beatles, most rock groups were quartets consisting of drums, lead guitar, rhythm guitar, and bass guitar. The guy with the nicest guitar and the most knowledge of music got to be lead guitar. That was me. The other guitarists had to be content with rhythm and bass. However, there was a problem with me being lead guitar. I wanted to sound like George Harrison, the Beatles lead guitarist, but I sounded like a jazz guitarist instead. Fortunately, I learned, little by little, to play rock'n'roll. As I improved on the guitar, my musical tastes became broader. I became interested in learning to play classical guitar.

I bought my first classical guitar about ten years after I had started learning to play guitar. My classical was the work of an old Italian instrument maker in New York City. He put a lot of love into the instrument, and I learned to appreciate the music that guitar was meant to play such as the music of Bach, Vivaldi, and Villa-Lobos. From that time on, I began to teach myself how to play the classical guitar. To this day, I am still learning. I try to play my Segovia etudes often, and every Christmastime I work on my version of Bach's "Jesu, Joy of Man's Desiring."

In addition to my continued study of classical guitar, I have come back to the jazz music that my guitar teachers tried to teach me years ago. When I played rock'n'roll, I used to think that jazz was boring. Now it is a never-ending source of creative guitar playing for me. I guess if I had to label myself as a guitarist, I would call myself a jazz guitarist. I have learned the songs of some great American jazz songwriters such as George Gershwin, Cole Porter, Duke Ellington, and Fats Waller. My guitar has been my passport to different musical worlds, and each world has offered me a different musical culture. Lately, I have become interested in Irish music and traditional North American dance music. My trusted companion on all these new musical journeys has been my guitar. It is always at hand. I do not travel for long periods of time without it. When I think of other hobbies, I can't help but feel I am very lucky to have taken up the guitar. It has been one of the joys of my life.

Answer these questions about the essay.

1. Write **introduction, body,** or **conclusion** next to each paragraph in the essay. How many body paragraphs are there in this essay?

   _____

2. Underline the sentence in the introduction that tells the general subject of the essay. (This is called the **topic.** We will study about it in the next unit.)

3. Underline two times the sentence(s) in the introduction that give(s) the main idea of the essay. (This is called the **thesis.** You will study about it in the next unit.)

4. What do you think are the purposes of the introduction? What does a writer do in the first paragraph?

   _____

   _____

5. Circle the transition or topic sentence for each body paragraph.

6. Put parentheses ( ) around each detail, supporting idea or example in the body paragraphs.

7. Underline what you think is the most important sentence in the concluding paragraph.

8. What do you think is the main purpose of the conclusion? What does the writer do in the conclusion?

_____

_____

9. What do you like about the essay?

_____

_____

Activity 5: Writing the Introduction and Conclusion

For many writers, writing the *body* of an academic essay is easier than writing the introduction and conclusion. Why? Because the body is where all of your information is. Writing the introduction and conclusion may require more creativity to make interesting paragraphs. At the same time, the introduction and conclusion are **very** important because they are the first and last impressions that your reader will have.

The Introduction

Purpose: 1. Get the reader's attention.
2. Introduce the topic.
3. State the thesis (main idea or point of view).
4. Orient the reader to your method of development.

Techniques:

Here are some ways for getting the reader's attention (see examples on the opposite page).

- Begin with a question.
- Begin with a general statement.
- Begin with a surprising statistic or fact.
- Begin with a famous quotation or proverb.
- Begin with a short personal story.
- Begin with a historical reference or refer to a current event.

Dangers to avoid:

Don't try to say everything in the introduction. Save your details for the body.

Don't write "My topic is . . ." or "I'm going to write about . . ."

Examples of techniques to get the reader's attention in the introduction.

Topic: Recreation

- Begin with a question.
  What do you do in your spare time?

- Begin with a general statement.
  Everyone has a favorite leisure activity.

- Begin with a surprising statistic or fact.
  People who know how to relax live longer.

- Begin with a famous quotation or proverb.
  "All work and no play makes Jack a dull boy." The same is true for Jane.

- Begin with a short personal story.
  Last summer, while driving across the United States, I thought about the importance of vacations.

- Begin with a historical reference or refer to a current event.
  For hundreds of years, families have been packing suitcases and taking vacations.

The Conclusion

The conclusion is the last place for you to make your point. It is the last impression your reader has. Unfortunately, many writers run out of steam.

Techniques:

- Summarize your main points or main idea.
- End with a question.
- End with a famous quotation that illustrates your point.
- Ask for the reader to do something related to the topic.

Dangers to avoid:

Don't make your conclusion too short.

Don't use the same words as you used in the introduction when you summarize.

Don't write "The End."

Don't introduce new ideas that you didn't develop in the body of your essay.

For the following topic and thesis, use three different techniques to make an interesting introduction.

Topic: Movies

Thesis: Many people around the world watch movies as a regular form of recreation.

1. _____

   _____

   _____

   _____

   _____

   _____

   _____

2. _____

   _____

   _____

   _____

   _____

   _____

   _____

3. _____

   _____

   _____

   _____

   _____

   _____

   _____

Writing and Revising Assignment: A Dream Vacation

Work in groups of four students. Imagine that you have won a contest! Your prize is a 24-HOUR DREAM VACATION! You can go anywhere and do anything. Don't worry about money; all expenses will be paid by your college. You can plan a trip to one place, but why not go to more than one place. Your only limitation is time and distance. For example, it would be impossible to go to Paris, Bali, and Rio de Janeiro and come home in one day.

Step 1: In your group, decide where you want to go for the morning, afternoon, and night. Take notes. Organize your notes by the three parts of the day.

Step 2: Talk about details and continue taking notes. How you will get to each place (car, private jet, limo)? What will you wear? Where will you eat? What will you do? Remember, the more details you have, the more interesting your writing will be.

Step 3: Now work individually. Write the first draft of your three **body paragraphs.** Think about what verb tense you will use. It will be easier to write in the past tense. You can write about your dream vacation as if you have already returned from it. Be sure to put transition sentences between each paragraph. **Do not write the introduction or conclusion yet.**

Step 4: Exchange paragraphs in your group. Read the paragraphs of the other students. Make notes on the bottom of their papers. Write (a) what you like best (b) what is not clear and (c) what other information should be included.

Step 5: Read the comments on your own paper. Edit your body paragraphs.

Step 6: Write an introductory and concluding paragraph.

Step 7: Again have someone from your group read your introductory and concluding paragraphs. Are they clear? Are they interesting?

Step 8: Rewrite your essay and submit it to your teacher.

ADDITIONAL PRACTICE

A. Vocabulary Expansion (Vocabulary)

Fill in the blanks with words related to leisure and recreation activities.

A _____   N _____

B _____   O _____

C _____   P _____

D _____   Q _____

E _____   R _____

F _____   S _____

G _____   T _____

H _____   U _____

I _____   V _____

J _____   W _____

K _____   X _____

L _____   Y _____

M _____   Z _____

B. Giving Examples (Structure)

Write sentences with the following words. Be careful with punctuation. Refer to page 109 for examples.

1. such as / winter sports

   _____

   _____

2. such as / summer sports

   _____

   _____

3. for example / places for a date

_____

_____

4. for example / places to take your mother when she visits

_____

_____

5. for instance / ways to travel (transportation)

_____

_____

6. for instance / kinds of music

_____

_____

C. Editing for Fragments and Run-ons: Review (Structure)

Read this paragraph. Write it again, correcting the fragments and
run-on sentences.

My last day off was wonderful. Because my brother lent me his car. I took
my friends to the mall to go shopping. We had a lot of things to buy because the
holidays are coming. First, we went to look for a gift for my mother. It's easy to
find something special for her. For example, something for the house or a blouse
or a sweater. We found just the perfect gift it wasn't too expensive either.
We kept on shopping for hours. We ate a lot of fast food. For instance, coffee,
donuts, and hamburgers. We came home with our pockets empty. But we felt
happy it was a great day.

_____

_____

_____

_____

_____

_____

_____

_____

D. Reading Reviews (Vocabulary)

Most newspapers feature reviews of movies, plays, music, books, and restaurants. They're usually interesting reading, a good way to increase your vocabulary, and a good source of ideas on how to spend your leisure time.

Cut out a review from a newspaper or a magazine and read it carefully. Be sure it is a review and not an advertisement. On the next page, fill out the chart about the review.

Source (Name of newspaper or magazine, date)	
Subject (What was reviewed/name of movie, restaurant etc.)	
Reviewer's Opinion Complimentary (positive), critical (negative), or mixed	
Positive Words in the Review	
Negative Words in the Review	
Your Comment or Opinion (about the movie or restaurant, etc.)	

Bring the review to class and summarize it for your group. Use the chart above to help you explain it.

E. Writing Reviews (Writing/Vocabulary)

Read these three sample reviews. Then, choose a movie, restaurant, book, or song and write your own review.

The best movie of the year by far is *Like Water for Chocolate.* It has all of the elements of a great movie: humor, love, tragedy, magic, and beauty. Beauty is the key word. The actors are beautiful. The camera work is beautiful. The story and the language are beautiful. The movie is in Spanish, but people who don't understand Spanish can read the English subtitles. Don't forget to bring tissues for this movie. You'll laugh, sigh, and cry. You may even get hungry. If you only see one movie in the 1990s, be sure to see this one.

Are you tired of your own cooking? Are you looking for the perfect place for your next date? Do you want to take your family out to dinner? Then cash your paycheck and go to the China Castle on Friday night. The menu is as big as a book! I recommend a combination dinner for the most variety. The service is fast and friendly. You may even be served by a classmate! I was. The atmosphere is festive. You can choose to sit by a window or in a booth. If you go, don't be surprised if you see me there with my family.

If you want to taste some authentic Mexican food, don't go to *Tacos de Mi Mama.* The dinner I had was a real disappointment. The food was served cold, and it was tasteless, not at all like the Mexican dishes my mother makes. The atmosphere was terrible. There weren't enough waiters and waitresses, so we had to wait a long time to place our order. I wouldn't recommend this restaurant to anyone!

UNIT FIVE JOURNAL TOPIC SUGGESTIONS

Here are some journal topics for the theme of this unit. Choose any
or all of them to write about in your journal.

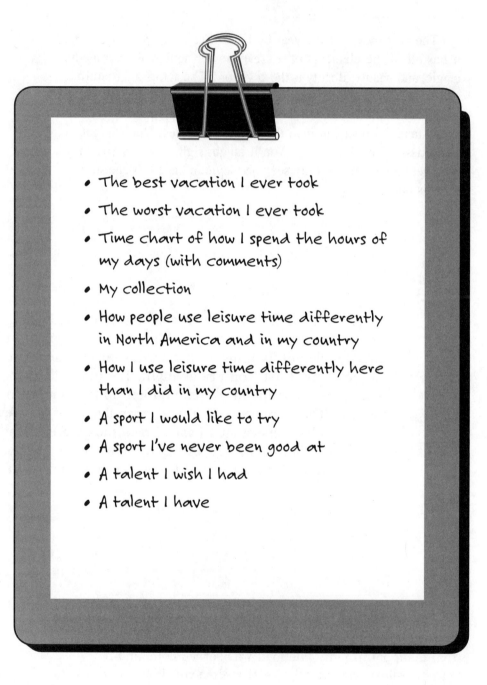

- The best vacation I ever took
- The worst vacation I ever took
- Time chart of how I spend the hours of my days (with comments)
- My collection
- How people use leisure time differently in North America and in my country
- How I use leisure time differently here than I did in my country
- A sport I would like to try
- A sport I've never been good at
- A talent I wish I had
- A talent I have

UNIT FIVE VOCABULARY LOG

Write new vocabulary words here. Write a sentence for each word showing
that you understand the meaning and can use the word correctly.

UNIT SIX

THE NATURAL WORLD

MY FAVORITE PLACE

PART I — PREWRITING

Activity 1: Painting a Picture in Words

A. Write down as many names of things as you can for Picture One on the opposite page.

_____

_____

_____

_____

_____

B. With a partner, talk about Picture One. Describe as precisely as you can what you see in the picture. Take turns giving your descriptions until you have talked about everything you can.

Activity 2: Comparing Experience

Work with a partner. Ask each other questions about the scene in Picture Two on the opposite page. Write down any new words or expressions that you learn from your partner.

EXAMPLES: *Have you ever been hiking in the mountains?*
Where have you been on your hikes?
Did you ever see a wild animal on your hikes?

Activity 3: Scientific Language

A. Read this scientific explanation of why a rose is red. Focus on what language is used to make the explanation scientific.

Why Is a Rose Red?

"Roses are red and violets are blue" are the words to a children's rhyme. Why is a rose red? Someone might think that a rose is red because that is its color. However, a rose is red because that is the color of the spectrum it reflects.

Color is the effect that is produced on the eye and the nerves in the eye by light waves. The nerve cells in the retina of the eye that are sensitive to the different wavelengths of light are called rods and cones. Light stimulates different color cones, making perception of color possible.

Each light wave of color has a different wavelength. The spectrum of color is red, orange, yellow, green, blue, indigo, and violet. When light falls on an object, some of it is absorbed, and some of it is reflected. The color of an object depends on the wavelength that it reflects. A red object observed in daylight appears red because it reflects only the waves producing red light. A red rose is red because it reflects the red wavelength in daylight.

B. Think about nature. Can you explain to your classmates why things look as they do or how things happen? Think of something in nature that you would like to explain to your classmates. Then, form groups of four and take turns saying what you know about your subject.

For homework, go to the library and find a science book or a reference book. Look up your subject. Take notes. Be sure you don't just copy the exact words from the book. Explain what you have learned about your subject in your group during the next class.

Here are some things in nature that you might explain.

a blue sky   honey
an elephant's trunk   rising and falling tides
autumn leaves   thunder and lightning
clouds   waves

Subject: _____

Reference Book: _____

Notes: _____

_____

_____

_____

_____

_____

_____

_____

_____

_____

_____

_____

_____

_____

_____

_____

PART II — STRUCTURE

Activity 1: Using *also*, *then*, and *on the other hand*

Use *also* to express a second idea which is similar to the first one you wrote.

EXAMPLE: I have been going to the beach for years. I have **also** been hiking in the mountains for a long time.

Use **then** to link two ideas by time order, the second coming after the first.

EXAMPLE: I went to the Grand Canyon. **Then** I crossed the Mojave Desert.

Use *on the other hand* when you want to contrast two ideas that are opposite or very different from each other.

EXAMPLE: Some people say fall is the prettiest season of the year. **On the other hand,** others say that spring is the prettiest.

Notice that these words show relationships between sentences but **do not** combine sentences.

	SENTENCE COMBINING CHART: UNIT 6			
RELATIONSHIP	**INDEPENDENT AND INDEPENDENT CLAUSE**	**DEPENDENT AND INDEPENDENT CLAUSE**	**INDEPENDENT AND INDEPENDENT CLAUSE**	**INDEPENDENT AND INDEPENDENT CLAUSE**
ADDITION	, and			also
CAUSE AND EFFECT	, so	because	; therefore,	
CONTRAST	, but	although even though though	; however,	on the other hand,
CHOICE	, or			
TIME		before • after as soon as since • when while • whenever		then • next

SENTENCE COMBINING CHART: EXAMPLE SENTENCES

RELATIONSHIP	INDEPENDENT AND INDEPENDENT CLAUSE	DEPENDENT AND INDEPENDENT CLAUSE	INDEPENDENT AND INDEPENDENT CLAUSE	INDEPENDENT AND INDEPENDENT CLAUSE
ADDITION	I can sing well, **and** I can play the guitar like a professional.			I can sing well. I **also** can play the guitar like a professional.
CAUSE AND EFFECT	It rained, **so** the picnic was cancelled.	**Because** it rained, the picnic was cancelled. The picnic was cancelled **because** it rained.	It rained; **therefore,** the picnic was cancelled. It rained. **Therefore,** the picnic was cancelled.	
CONTRAST	I tried, **but** I couldn't understand.	**Although** I tried, I couldn't understand. I couldn't understand. **even though** I tried.	I tried; **however,** I couldn't understand. I tried. **However,** I couldn't understand.	
CHOICE	You can do it now, **or** I will do it later.			You can do it now. **On the other hand,** you can do it later.
TIME		**When** he arrived, I left. I have been here **since** the room opened.		I got up. **Then** I took a shower.

Note: There are many more ways to combine sentences in English. These are only the ways practiced in this text.

Combine these sentences using *also, then,* or *on the other hand.*

1. Carlos has been a member of the Sierra Club for two years. Carlos has been a member of Greenpeace since 1990.

   _____

   _____

   _____

2. Pat studied botany in college. She worked in a plant nursery during those four years.

   _____

   _____

   _____

3. Dung flew across the Pacific Ocean when he was a high school student. He flew across the Atlantic the year he graduated from college.

   _____

   _____

   _____

4. Helene and Alex climbed Mt. McKinley alone. They tried to climb Mt. Everest by themselves.

   _____

   _____

   _____

5. Palm trees are native to California. The eucalyptus tree was brought to California from Australia.

   _____

   _____

   _____

6. Arturo and Ji Yun plan to surf in Hawaii if they can save a lot of money. If they are broke, they will just go camping in the Sierras instead.

   _____

   _____

   _____

Activity 2: Describing the Geography of Your Country

A. Find your country on a map of the world. Show your classmates where it is. Tell them what countries are next to your own.

B. Write six sentences with *also, then,* and *on the other hand* to describe the geography of your country. You might want to use some of the words listed here and other words that your teacher and classmates think of using.

mountains	plain	seaport
rivers	desert	volcano
lakes	jungle	delta
forest	valley	hills

EXAMPLES: The northwestern United States has a wet climate and a lot of large forests.
On the other hand, the southwestern U.S. has a dry climate with a lot of deserts.

If you like seaports, you should visit New York or Boston. Then, try Miami or New Orleans for warmer weather.

Hawaii is the only American state with jungle. It is also one of the few states with an active volcano.

1. _____

_____

2. _____

_____

3. _____

_____

4. _____

_____

5. _____

_____

6. _____

_____

Activity 3: Comparing Natural Scenes

Look back at Pictures One and Two at the beginning of this unit. Use *also,*
then, and on *the other hand* to compare the pictures. Work with a partner.
Write at least six sentences comparing the two pictures.

_____

_____

_____

_____

_____

_____

_____

_____

_____

_____

_____

PART III — WRITING AND EDITING

Activity 1: Reading and Analyzing an Essay

A. Read this essay carefully.

Morning on the Beach

I suppose that everyone has a favorite place. Mine is the beach. I don't mean the beach of umbrellas, suntan lotion, Frisbees, and radios. That is afternoon on the beach when every patch of sand is covered by blankets and chairs, and you can't hear the sea, only people talking. I mean morning on the beach. I try to get up as early as I can and walk the beach silently. There are no people in the early morning, only sandpipers, seals, pelicans, and hermit crabs. At that time of day, the quiet insistence of the waves which beat against the shore makes me calm inside. I get a feeling of peace and strength from gazing out to the water, knowing that waves came to shore before I was here and will come to shore after I am gone.

I have often walked the beach on winter mornings just before sunrise. The morning sky looks like a palette of watercolors, though mostly blues, purples, grays, and yellows. When the sun comes over the horizon and brings the morning light, I can feel the meaning of the new day. It has really begun! The sun says so, and that is about as high an authority as I can think of. The sun gives more than morning light. It also brings warmth to the day and takes the sting out of the shore breeze. I share the sunrise with sandpipers and seagulls, who seem to be constantly looking for food at the water's edge. Every time I see a sandpiper I am reminded of a Japanese haiku poem in which "Sandpipers chase the sea and turning are chased back again." I love that image because I know it so well.

Sometimes I get lucky on my morning walks and come across a seal who has decided to come to shore. Almost always, the seal has chosen a spot far away from the paths which lead down to the beach from the cliffs above. Almost always, the seal comes in at high tide when the water nearly covers the whole shoreline. I try to do two things when I spot a seal. One is to get closer so that I can see him better, and the second is to move slowly and silently so that I won't disturb him. Usually, the seal has found a perch on a small boulder and is intent on grooming himself in the early sunlight. Usually, he sees me no matter how quiet I think I am, and with a bark or two in my direction, he slides back into the water and out of sight. However, just the minute or two for which I could look at him is enough to make me happy and somehow make that day special. I didn't see the seal in a zoo, clapping his flippers for fish. I saw him as he is in the natural world, a seal, not an entertainer.

There are times when I see seals and other creatures of the sea that make me very sad. It often happens like this. I am walking along the shoreline and I spot a large object. It doesn't look like a rock or a boat. I get a feeling inside that the object doesn't belong on the beach where it is because I know the contours of the shoreline so well. I come closer. I see gulls near the object. I start to smell something. It is the smell of decay. A hundred feet or so before I reach the object, I know it is a dead seal. I walk up to it to inspect the carcass. I see that around its neck is some sort of fishing net. Its body is swollen and its stomach has been ripped open by gulls. I know that seals like humans must die. What upsets me, though, is the thought that the seal might have died as a result of getting trapped in a fishing net. It might have drowned in its own element, water. Fortunately for me, these times of sad discoveries are few. Most of the time I am happy when I walk on the beach in the morning.

What is it that makes the beach such a special place for me? I was born and raised in New York City, in the concrete and asphalt of city life. Therefore, you couldn't say it was because of my childhood surroundings. On the other hand, my family used to spend summers in the country on an island with lots of beaches. I still remember those times and I cherish them. Another reason for my love of beaches might be that a few

miles from my boyhood home was the city shoreline with its docks, ferries, and tankers. I could never swim in those waters or lie in what little sand there was, but I could look out into the waves and dream. Perhaps I was dreaming of the beaches I would one day walk on another coast.

B. Answer the following questions about the essay. Circle the letter of the best choice.

1. Which of the following do you think is the **topic** of the essay?
    a. New York City, my hometown
    b. my favorite time and place
    c. the best beaches of the world
    d. the animals at the beach

2. Which sentence do you think states the main idea of the essay? (This is called the **thesis.**)

   a. I suppose that everyone has a favorite place.

   b. My favorite place is morning on the beach.

   c. There are times when I see seals and other creatures of the sea that make me very sad.

   d. Perhaps I was dreaming of the beaches I would one day walk on another coast.

3. In the second paragraph, what idea about the beach does the author focus on?

   a. the beach is lonely

   b. birds on the beach

   c. Japanese poems

   d. morning on the beach in winter

4. In paragraph three, why does the author write about seals?

   a. they are in the zoo and on the beach

   b. they are free and happy at the beach

   c. they are entertainers

   d. seals are afraid of people

5. In paragraph four, how does the author feel?

   a. happy

   b. trapped

   c. sad

   d. fortunate

6. Why does the author write about the dead seal?

   a. because you can be happy or sad in your favorite place

   b. because seals are dangerous

   c. because gulls are near the object

   d. because it doesn't look like a rock or a boat

7. What is it that makes the beach a special place for the author?

   a. He used to spend summers at the beach, and he lived near a harbor.

   b. He grew up in an area of concrete and asphalt.

   c. He could never swim in the water near his house.

   d. He was born in New York City.

Activity 2: Topic vs. Thesis

By now you know that every paragraph needs to have a main idea or focus and usually a topic sentence. In an academic essay, the writer usually puts the main idea of the entire essay in the introductory paragraph. This main idea sentence for the whole essay is called a **thesis.** It expresses the author's point of view or opinion about the topic. The thesis may be more than one sentence. It often appears at the *end* of the introductory paragraph.

Every topic can have many different theses.

EXAMPLE: Topic: my favorite place

Thesis: My favorite place is the beach in the morning.
My favorite place is a nightclub in a big city.
My favorite place is a ski slope.

Write a thesis for each of these topics.

1. the most beautiful place in the world

   _____

2. pollution

   _____

3. cities

   _____

4. endangered animals

   _____

5. pesticides and food additives

   _____

Activity 3: The Thesis

Sometimes a thesis gives the writer's opinion or point of view about the topic and more. It can also tell how the essay will be organized. For example: *I think a luxury cruise is the most relaxing kind of vacation.*

EXAMPLE: I have three favorite places. (This essay will probably have five paragraphs): Introduction

Paragraph about 1st favorite place: the house I grew up in
Paragraph about 2nd favorite place: my grandmother's kitchen
Paragraph about 3rd favorite place: my town square
Conclusion

Make an outline like the one in the example for the following thesis statements.

1. *We have three kinds of pollution to worry about in the world today.*

———————————————————————
———————————————————————
———————————————————————
———————————————————————
———————————————————————
———————————————————————
———————————————————————
———————————————————————
———————————————————————

2. *I know four vacation places where you can enjoy nature.*

———————————————————————
———————————————————————
———————————————————————
———————————————————————
———————————————————————
———————————————————————
———————————————————————
———————————————————————
———————————————————————

Activity 4: Editing an Essay

You are an editor at a magazine called *Nature*. Your boss has told you to edit this essay "Morning on the Beach." She says it's too long for the space she has left in the magazine. She has told you to cut out at least one sentence per paragraph if you can, and combine any sentences that you can. She has also said that she would like you to use *also, then,* and *on the other hand* in your editing of this essay. Can you do it?

1. Reread the essay and decide on a line in each paragraph that you could cut out. Discuss your decision with a classmate. Then, **with a pencil,** put a light line through the sentence you have decided to cut.

2. Look at the essay again. This time, decide which sentences could be combined using any connecting words you know. Again discuss your ideas with a classmate. Then, **below the essay,** rewrite the combined form of the sentences you have chosen.

3. Now, once more, look at the essay. Are there any places where you could follow your boss's wish and use *also, then,* or *on the other hand?* If you can find a place to use one of these words and phrases, rewrite the sentence or sentences below in number three. (*Hint:* you might have to change some of the words in the essay.)

Morning on the Beach

1

1 I suppose that everyone has a favorite place. Mine is the beach. I don't mean
2 the beach of umbrellas, suntan lotion, Frisbees, and radios. That is afternoon on
3 the beach when every patch of sand is covered by blankets and chairs, and you
4 can't hear the sea, only people talking. I mean morning on the beach. I try to
5 get up as early as I can and walk the beach silently. There are no people in the
6 early morning, only sandpipers, seals, pelicans, and hermit crabs. At that time
7 of day, the quiet insistence of the waves which beat against the shore makes
8 me calm inside. I get a feeling of peace and strength from gazing out to the
9 water, knowing that waves came to shore before I was here and will come to
10 shore after I am gone.

2

1 I have often walked the beach on winter mornings just before sunrise. The
2 morning sky looks like a palette of watercolors, though mostly blues, purples,
3 grays, and yellows. When the sun comes over the horizon and brings the
4 morning light, I can feel the meaning of the new day. It has really begun! The sun
5 says so, and that is about as high an authority as I can think of. The sun gives
6 more than morning light. It also brings warmth to the day and takes the sting out
7 of the shore breeze. I share the sunrise with sandpipers and seagulls, who seem
8 to be constantly looking for food at the water's edge. Every time I see a sandpiper
9 I am reminded of a Japanese haiku poem in which "Sandpipers chase the sea and
10 turning are chased back again." I love that image because I know it so well.

3

1   Sometimes I get lucky on my morning walks and come across a seal who has
2   decided to come to shore. Almost always, the seal has chosen a spot far away
3   from the paths which lead down to the beach from the cliffs above. Almost always,
4   the seal comes in at high tide when the water nearly covers the whole shoreline.
5   I try to do two things when I spot a seal. One is to get closer so that I can see him
6   better, and the second is to move slowly and silently so that I won't disturb him.
7   Usually, the seal has found a perch on a small boulder and is intent on grooming
8   himself in the early sunlight. Usually, he sees me no matter how quiet I think I am,
9   and with a bark or two in my direction, he slides back into the water and out of
10   sight. However, just the minute or two for which I could look at him is enough to
11   make me happy and somehow make that day special. I didn't see the seal in a
12   zoo, clapping his flippers for fish. I saw him as he is in the natural world, a
13   seal, not an entertainer.

4

1   There are times when I see seals and other creatures of the sea that make me
2   very sad. It often happens like this. I am walking along the shoreline and I spot a
3   large object. It doesn't look like a rock or a boat. I get a feeling inside that the
4   object doesn't belong on the beach where it is because I know the contours of the
5   shoreline so well. I come closer. I see gulls near the object. I start to smell
6   something. It is the smell of decay. A hundred feet or so before I reach the object,
7   I know it is a dead seal. I walk up to it to inspect the carcass. I see that around its
8   neck is some sort of fishing net. Its body is swollen and its stomach has been
9   ripped open by gulls. I know that seals like humans must die. What upsets me,
10   though, is the thought that the seal might have died as a result of getting trapped
11   in a fishing net. It might have drowned in its own element, water. Fortunately
12   for me, these times of sad discoveries are few. Most of the time I am happy
13   when I walk on the beach in the morning.

5

1   What is it that makes the beach such a special place for me? I was born and
2   raised in New York City, in the concrete and asphalt of city life. Therefore, you
3   couldn't say it was because of my childhood surroundings. On the other hand, my
4   family used to spend summers in the country on an island with lots of beaches.
5   I still remember those times and I cherish them. Another reason for my love of
6   beaches might be that a few miles from my boyhood home was the city shoreline
7   with its docks, ferries, and tankers. I could never swim in those waters or lie in
8   what little sand there was, but I could look out into the waves and dream. Perhaps
9   I was dreaming of the beaches I would one day walk on another coast.

1. Did you draw a line through a sentence in each paragraph?

2. Write your combined sentences here.

_____

_____

_____

_____

_____

_____

_____

_____

_____

3. Write your new sentence with *also, then,* or *on the other hand* here.

_____

_____

_____

_____

_____

_____

_____

_____

_____

PART IV — WRITING AND REVISING ASSIGNMENT

Writing Assignment: My Favorite Place

Step 1: Return to Picture Four, which is blank, at the beginning of this unit. In that space, draw as well as you can your favorite place in nature. Put as much detail as you can into the drawing.

Step 2: Work with a partner. Each of you describe your favorite place. As you listen to your partner, look at his or her picture. Can you think of other words and other ways to describe what you see? Tell your partner.

Step 3: Write a description of your drawing.

Step 4: Write a thesis statement. Add it to your description.

Step 5: Brainstorm ways to expand your writing from paragraph to essay. What categories will you choose? How many paragraphs will they form? Ideally, there will be five paragraphs in your essay.

1. An introductory paragraph with the thesis statement in it
2. Category one
3. Category two
4. Category three
5. A conclusion with restatement of the thesis

Step 6: Write a first draft of your essay.

Revising Assigment

Step 1: Make three copies of your essay to hand out to three classmates who will work with you on revision of your essay. Ask your classmates to read your essay for homework. Ask them to put a line through sentences that they think you could cut and to write at least three examples of sentences you could join. (They can write on your essay copy at the bottom.) At least one of the combined sentences should use *also, then,* or *on the other hand.*

Step 2: In class, work with one group member at a time and share your ideas about revising to make the essay better. Spend ten minutes with each person. At the end of the class, give each person his or her copy back with your ideas for cuts and combinations, plus any other ideas you might have for revision.

Step 3: At home, use your classmate's suggestions to revise your own essay. Bring it in the next day, and read it to the group. Take ten minutes to read and discuss the revisions. Take notes on any further ideas your classmates give you.

*A*DDITIONAL *P*RACTICE

A. Describing (Prewriting)

Describe these well-known natural places and phenomena to a classmate.

1. Mt. Everest
2. Mars
3. the sun
4. the Amazon River
5. Mount Fuji
6. the Grand Canyon
7. the North Pole
8. Tahiti
9. the Yucatan
10. Niagara Falls

B. Writing Descriptive Sentences (Writing)

Write down the names of some famous natural places in your country.
Write a sentence about each one.

_____

_____

_____

_____

_____

_____

_____

_____

_____

_____

_____

_____

_____

_____

_____

C. Freewriting (Prewriting)

In five minutes, write as much as you can on the topic, "Pollution."

_____

_____

_____

_____

_____

_____

_____

_____

_____

_____

_____

_____

_____

_____

_____

_____

_____

_____

_____

_____

_____

_____

D. Using *on the other hand* (Structure)

Write five controversial sentences like the example. Then exchange papers with a classmate. Write contrasting sentences for your partner's sentences.

EXAMPLE: a. Nuclear energy is relatively clean and inexpensive.

b. On the other hand, it is very dangerous.

1a. _____

_____

1b. _____

_____

2a. _____

_____

2b. _____

_____

3a. _____

_____

3b. _____

_____

4a. _____

_____

4b. _____

_____

5a. _____

_____

5b. _____

_____

E. Run-ons and Fragments (Structure and Editing)

Read the following sentences carefully. Mark each **RO** for run-on, **F** for fragment, or **CS** for complete sentence. Correct each incorrect sentence.

1. _____ Many zoos are well run, on the other hand, some zoos are poorly designed for animals.

_____

_____

2. _____ Dusk in the desert can be a spectacular sight, also dawn.

_____

_____

3. _____ I spent a week at the beach, then I went to the mountains.

_____

_____

4. _____ Many people today depend on private automobiles for transportation, therefore air pollution is a problem in big cities.

_____

_____

5. _____ When it snows.

_____

_____

6. _____ There are many ways to learn about animals.

_____

_____

7. _____ The sun is necessary for life, but it can also be dangerous.

_____

_____

8. _____ The U.S. National Park Service oversees several beautiful parks. For example, Yosemite.

_____

_____

UNIT SIX JOURNAL TOPIC SUGGESTIONS

Here are some journal topics for the theme of this unit. Choose any
or all of them to write about in your journal.

- How I take care of the environment
- What animal I am most like
- My fantasy landscape (a cave, a
  waterfall, a garden, etc.)
- How I feel about perfumes and air
  fresheners
- How Americans are (aren't) taking care
  of the environment
- How people in my country are (aren't)
  taking care of the environment
- How I imagine my country will be 100 years
  from now
- The best technological invention
- The worst technological invention
- What this city (town) needs to improve
  the quality of life

UNIT SIX VOCABULARY LOG

Write new vocabulary words here. Write a sentence for each word showing that you understand the meaning and can use the word correctly.

APPENDIX ONE — SAMPLE PAPER

SUGGESTIONS FOR SUCCESS IN COLLEGE WRITING CLASSES

All of your work should look professional.

Betty Mannion
Writing 119, M. Spaventa
Essay #6
May 15, 1997

My Favorite Place

In this hectic world everybody needs to relax, and most people look forward to enjoying their favorite place in their free time. My favorite place is my home.

My home is the only place where I can feel like a Queen in my own kingdom because in my home I make myself comfortable, powerful, and safe. I always do anything I want. At home I make all kinds of decisions about cleaning, shopping, cooking, and making plans for vacations. I love it.

Usually, every morning as soon as I clean my house carefully, I like to read the newspaper in my back yard. After everybody is gone, it's fantastic to have a little free time to enjoy the sun, drink some tea, and read the news in my quiet lovely home.

In my favorite place, the kitchen is my favorite room. I like to bake cookies, pies, and cakes. Also I'm always excited about experimenting with some new recipes. I really enjoy cooking because I try to give my family a gift of good meals. While I cook, I can see my beautiful garden and roses through my window. I love my kitchen. It's small but enough for me. I can't even wait until my son and my husband come home. Then we can have dinner together and talk about our day or discuss the current news. Right away after we finish dinner, I clean my kitchen while watching my husband and my son playing in the back yard.

Maybe for some people it sounds boring, but for me, my home is my favorite place. I love to see my kitchen and the rest of the house looking very clean. It makes me feel great when I spend a long time at home doing my best for my family and for the place where I live. It is the place where I enjoy the best I have: my family.

Notebooks and Homework Papers

1. Buy standard size paper (8 1/2 by 11 with lines) with three holes, and keep it in a binder.

2. Every paper *must have* a heading. Some teachers have a special style. If your teacher does not tell you how to head your paper, you can use this form.

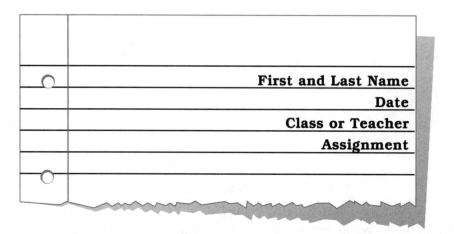

3. Don't write in the margins on the left and right side of the paper. (Most notebook paper has a red or blue line to show the margin.)

4. Some teachers want you to skip lines or write on every other line.

5. Your teacher will tell you if you should use pencil or pen. If you use pencil, make sure your teacher can see it! Use computers whenever you can.

Cheating and Plagiarism

Cheating and plagiarism are very serious matters in American classrooms! Please don't cheat or plagiarize.

Cheating = Looking at another student's paper for the answers on a quiz or test, or looking in your book or at papers or answers when you take a test.

Plagiarism = Copying the words from a book and presenting them as your own words. You need to use quotation marks ".." when you use the words from a book or someone else's words. Also, you cannot copy another student's essay or paper and put your name on it.

APPENDIX TWO — JOURNAL WRITING

Journals are notebooks in which writers keep a record of their ideas, opinions, and descriptions of daily life, and in which they allow their imagination and creativity to develop. In writing classes, instructors often direct students to do unedited writing and freewriting assignments in their journals, as well as to record their ideas, opinions, and observations.

Each writing instructor has different ideas about journal writing. Your instructor will tell you how to keep your journal, and will probably collect it at certain times during the semester. Your instructor might write reactions to what you have written and offer suggestions for vocabulary or for improving your grammar. However, the main point of keeping a journal is to give you a chance to write what you think without worrying about a grade or about being correct.

Journal writing is writing free from worries about vocabulary and grammar. Some instructors encourage their students to write in their own language as well as in English because it helps them say something they can't express in English.

Journal writing gives us a chance to exercise our *writing muscle*. Of course, there really is no such thing as a writing muscle, but the image is important to understand. In order to write well, we need to write often, just as in order to have strong, healthy muscles, we have to exercise them often. Both writing and muscles need an energy source for them to grow. For muscles, it is nutrition from the food we eat. For writing, our life experience and reading contribute to our writing. Good writers are people who read a lot. Therefore, your instructor may ask you to read something and then to write in your journal about what you have read.

Buy a standard size notebook with ruled lined paper. Make it your journal for this writing class only. Write nothing else in it: not other subjects, not other class assignments. The reward from keeping a journal, besides the informal conversation that takes place in it between you and yourself and you and your instructor, is that after the course is finished, you will have a record of what you read, what you experienced, and what you thought about during that time.

At the end of each unit, you will find some topics related to the theme of the unit. Write about them in your journal.

APPENDIX THREE — CAPITALIZATION

BASIC RULES

Capitalization in English is a set of conventions about which letters of words should be capitalized and which should not. Sometimes writers deliberately break these conventions so that readers will look at their words in a different way. For example, the American poet e. e. cummings some times used lowercase letters where most people would use capitals, for both his initials and his last name. However, as a person learning to write standard English, you need to pay attention to what is considered the *right way* to capitalize letters, even if it is the opposite from what you have learned in your first language.

The list of rules below is limited to common problems for students learning to write English as a Second Language. For a complete list of capitalization rules, you can consult an English dictionary or a style manual.

1. Capitalize the first word in a sentence.

   EXAMPLE: **G**orillas are animals that live in Africa.

2. Capitalize the pronoun *I*, but no other pronouns unless they begin a sentence.

   EXAMPLE: **I** found that **I** like to write.

3. Capitalize the first letter of the first word in quoted speech.

   EXAMPLE: She asked, "**W**ho is coming to dinner tonight?"

4. Capitalize the first letter of a noun when it goes with the specific name of a person, place, or thing.

   EXAMPLE: **S**ecretary **S**mith of the **U**nited **N**ations visited the **E**iffel **T**ower yesterday.

5. Capitalize every word except conjunctions (words like *and, but*), articles (*the, a, an*), and short prepositions (*in, on*) in the titles of books, movies, plays, magazines, and other written works.

   EXAMPLE: **F**innegan, the **H**ero
   Study in **B**lue and **G**reen

   But, if the conjunction, article, or preposition is the first word of a title, then you must capitalize it.

   EXAMPLE: **B**ut Not for You
   A Gloomy Afternoon
   In Springtime

6. Capitalize the names of languages, nationalities, countries, cities, towns, and villages.

   EXAMPLE: The **S**panish of **M**exicans from **E**l **S**itio in **Z**acatecas, **M**exico is different from the **S**panish of **S**paniards from **M**adrid.

APPENDIX FOUR — PUNCTUATION

BASIC RULES

Punctuation is the use of standard signs and marks to separate words into sentences, clauses, and phrases in order to clarify meaning. As readers, we are helped by punctuation because it puts boundaries around things and ideas that are closely related. Reading without punctuation is very difficult. Try this example:

> Years ago when I was living in Korea I met a young man whose nickname was Gandhi I was never sure why he had that nickname whether he chose it for himself or someone else gave it to him Physically he didn't remind me of Gandhi in the least but in terms of character I believe there was some similarity

Now, take a pencil and put in punctuation where you think it should go. When you do this, you are creating boundaries and you are creating a rhythm which any reader can use to help read and understand the writing.

Here are some rules for punctuation. As with capitalization, this is not a complete list of rules, but a list that focuses on common ESL writing errors. For a more complete list, consult a dictionary, a grammar book, or a style manual.

1. A period goes at the end of a sentence or after the last letter of an abbreviation.

    EXAMPLE: I received a letter from Mr. John Jones. The date was written Jan. 9th.

    Remember that a period does *not* come after a title.

2. Use a comma before conjunctions when they join two independent clauses.

    EXAMPLE: I tried calling Burt at his office, but nobody answered the phone.

3. Use a comma when a dependent clause comes first.

    EXAMPLE: After Marie filled out the application, she mailed it.

4. Use a comma to set off dates, addresses, and titles.

    EXAMPLE: Dr. John Lincoln, Professor of Modern Music, died at his home in Cleveland, Ohio on March 23, 1990.

5. Use a comma to separate words, phrases, and clauses in a series.

    EXAMPLE: Ilya likes mango, papaya, passion fruit, and guava.
    Herbert complained about the bad weather, his dreary office job, and his boring life.

The comma that comes before *and* is optional.

> **EXAMPLE:** If Hilda learns Swedish, if she dyes her hair blond, and if she grows another six inches, maybe somebody will believe she comes from Sweden.

6. Use a comma to separate adjectives that follow one another.

> **EXAMPLE:** It was an old, evil-smelling, dark, and frightening room.

7. Use a semicolon to separate two independent clauses when they are not joined by a coordinating conjunction (words like *and, but, so*) or when they are joined by a conjunctive adverb (words like *however, otherwise, moreover*).

> **EXAMPLE:** Nuvia loved to work with her hands; she was a marvelous seamstress.
>
> Il Bum had always wanted to travel to Niagara Falls; however, he had never had the time to make the trip.

8. Use a colon after the greeting in a business letter or a formal letter.

> **EXAMPLE:** Dear Dr. Skinner:

9. Use quotation marks to set off direct speech.

> **EXAMPLE:** Ernesto said, "Makiko, you look a lot like my sister, Rocio."

10. Use an apostrophe to indicate possession.

> **EXAMPLE:** That is Lou's guitar.

11. Use an apostrophe to show that a letter or letters is missing from a word.

> **EXAMPLE:** He couldn't have been here in '69.

APPENDIX FIVE — WRITER FEEDBACK SHEET

You can photocopy this page and use it when you want feedback on your writing.

When giving feedback to a classmate, read the writing and then check according to your opinion for each category. Where it says comment, you can write something to the writer if you want to.

	It's really good.	It's okay.	It needs work.
1. Focus	_____	_____	_____
Comment:			
2. Interest	_____	_____	_____
Comment:			
3. Title	_____	_____	_____
Comment:			
4. Topic sentence	_____	_____	_____
Comment:			
5. Details/ Development	_____	_____	_____
Comment:			
6. Conclusion	_____	_____	_____
Comment:			
7. Form	_____	_____	_____
Comment:			
8. Grammar	_____	_____	_____
Comment:			
9. Spelling	_____	_____	_____
Comment:			
10. Punctuation	_____	_____	_____
Comment:			

APPENDIX SIX — GLOSSARY

TERMS USED IN THIS TEXT

coordinating conjunctions (*and, but, so, or*) words that join independent clauses. Use a comma before coordinating conjunctions.

  EXAMPLE: I have read the book**, but** I haven't seen the movie.

dependent clause a group of words including a subject and verb, but not a complete sentence by itself. A dependent clause begins with a subordinator. It must be connected with an independent clause in written English.

  EXAMPLE: When I was a child, I loved to read.

edit to find and correct mistakes to improve your writing

essay an academic writing of more than one paragraph that expresses a point of view or explains something. Students in American colleges and universities are frequently required to write essays.

focus the main idea of a paragraph

freewriting writing without worrying about mistakes. The purpose is to express your ideas and write as fluently as possible. Freewriting is also called quickwriting.

independent clause a group of words including a subject and verb which is a complete sentence by itself; it can be connected to an dependent clause, or it can be connected to another independent clause.

  EXAMPLE: I love to read.
      When I was a child, **I loved to read.**
      I love to read, and **I enjoy writing.**

peer editing helping a classmate or friend improve her or his writing. A peer is your equal, in this case, a classmate.

revise to add ideas or cut ideas from your writing to make it more clear and focused. Revising is usually done before editing for grammar, spelling, and punctuation mistakes.

subordinating conjunction (conjunctive adverb) (*after, before, when, as soon as, since, while, whenever, because, although, even though, though*) words that introduce dependent clauses.

  EXAMPLE: When I was a child, I loved to read.
      Because I read so much, writing is easy for me.

title   the introductory phrase to a paragraph, essay, story, or book. It is usually not a complete sentence. The title should capture the reader's attention or imagination.

thesis   the main idea or point of view of an essay

topic   the main idea

topic sentence   the sentence that shows the main idea of a paragraph. It limits the focus of the paragraph.

transition   (*therefore, however*) a kind of conjunction. Transitions combine independent clause and independent clause with a semicolon. Transitions can also be used to relate two independent clauses with a period.

> **EXAMPLE:** I have worked through this entire text; **therefore,** my writing has improved.
>
> My writing has improved a lot. **However,** I know that I have even more to learn.